An Appetite For Fugum

CHRISTINE SMALLWOOD

An Appetite For *Puglia*

The People, The Places, The Food

Photography by Eddie Jacob

Research and author: Christine Smallwood
Jacket, book and location maps design: Grade Design Consultants, London
Inside cover map: Encompass Graphics

Specially commissioned photography: Eddie Jacob

First published in the United Kingdom in 2008 by:
Bonny Day Publishing Limited
Unit B, 15 Bell Yard Mews
Bermondsey Street
London SE1 3TY

Copyright © 2008 Christine Smallwood

British Library Cataloguing-in-Publication Data
A catalogue record for this book is available from the
British Library

ISBN-978-0-9550058-2-4

This book is printed on paper which is ECF.
Paper is Biodegradable and can be recycled.
Made from European trees from sustainable forests.

Printed in England by Gavin Martin Associates Limited.

Recipes

The recipes in this book are all typical of the food served in
their respective restaurants. The majority of these chefs rely on
taste, sight, instinct and experience more than recipes, and all
would encourage you to do likewise.

As one queried when I asked for specifics: "Why do you need
quantities? Use what you have to cook what you feel like, and
then tuck in. Cooking at home should be fun."

The recipes have been tested in domestic settings several times
and amended where helpful, but certainly the simpler recipes
should be treated as starting guidelines for your own culinary
creativity.

Food Photos

All recipe photos were taken on location in the restaurants
where the dishes were prepared and as they were served up.
No stylist was involved and no special effects were used.

Raw Fish

Raw fish is popular in Puglia but we strongly advise you to
exercise caution if choosing to try this local speciality. Although
fans of raw fish consider it to be one of the great food
experiences, there are many who prefer to play it safe and eat
only cooked fish. We recommend that you assess the risks and
make up your own mind.

Inclusion

No payment has secured an invitation to participate in this
book; a restaurateur could not buy inclusion and the publisher
did not pay anybody to take part. Evaluation of all restaurants
was carried out anonymously and the bill was paid. In the
course of follow-ups (interviews, photographic shoots, etc)
some refreshments were accepted free of charge.

Contents

Introduction

It's not easy to find the quintessential Puglia. The *trulli*, those small whitewashed dwellings with conical roofs, seem to have become the default image, but that is more than a little misleading. From the heights of the Gargano and Monte Sant'Angelo to coastal towns like Gallipoli, from the international and cosmopolitan port of Bari to the beautiful small fishing harbour of Trani, from the tourist magnets of Alberobello and Lecce to the lower profile places such as Conversano and Orsara di Puglia, it's a large, long and varied region.

Those searching for the true Puglia may, however, find it, not in its towns and buildings, but in its people and its food. Certainly, if the warm welcome is one of the most appealing aspects of visiting Italy, the people in Puglia do all that they can to make theirs reach the temperature of the hottest *Mezzogiorno* summer days. And that's pretty warm. We lost count of the number of times we asked passing locals for directions and were cheerfully told that it would be easier if they showed us personally, hopping in their cars or walking out of their way to ensure we reached our destination.

And food is another major theme throughout the region. The Pugliesi don't just want you to eat up, they want you to savour their *territorio*. And they'll keep on feeding you with an eagerness bordering on the fanatical. It's a region that does not scrimp on portion size. Its renowned antipasti platters comprise serious quantities of food — and that's just the beginning. Could it be the sea air? Who knows, but they have healthy appetites down south.

If food and the people who produce it say something important about a region, then it's worth finding out where the finest examples of both can be found — and that is what we have tried to do here. Puglia's sheer size means that this book is forced to omit some treasures: Taranto, Ostuni, Barletta, Ruvo di Puglia, Cisternino and Otranto among many others all have their own charms and merits. Here, however, is a series of portraits presenting some of the most interesting characters behind some of the best food in Puglia.

But that is not to say that they have all been cut from the same template. There are upmarket restaurants such as L'Osteria Già Sotto L'Arco in Carovigno alongside casual places such as Antichi Sapori in Montegrosso. There are shining beacons of traditional cooking such as Cucina Casereccia in Lecce, while others, like Al Fornello da Ricci in Ceglie Messapica, judiciously select from outside influences to move their traditions forward. Peppe Zullo in his eponymous restaurant in Orsara di Puglia produces most of the raw ingredients he serves up, whereas others, including Antonello Magistà at Pasha in Conversano, are diligent about sourcing from the best producers in their area, and Pasquale Centrone of Da Tuccino in Polignano a Mare travels daily from one coast to the other to ensure he has the best fish available.

Some places are modern and stylish, like Il Pane e le Rose in Bari and Miseriaenobiltà in Alberobello, while others are more traditional, like Torrente Antico in Trani or de la Poste, Locanda in Andria. Nor did everyone here follow a direct route to their present employment: Beppe Schino of PerBacco in Bari was previously an architect, Aldo Massimo in Foggia a radiographer and Anna Ancona of Il Ritrovo degli Amici in Martina Franca a designer.

All of them, however, have an enthusiasm and commitment — and a very Pugliesi hint of the playful — that makes them notable examples of the region's love of food and hospitality. There perhaps you will find the quintessential Puglia. We hope you enjoy and are inspired by the stories of the people in this book.

Buon Viaggio! Buon Appetito!

Alberobello

The world's capital of *trulli*, the intriguing conical roofed dwellings, is swarming with visitors for most of the year. Whether you regard Alberobello as a delightful place and its *trulli* experience extraordinary, or feel it may have overdone the tourism angle, chances are that you'll feel obliged to join them at least briefly.

Miseriaenobiltà Franco Lacatena

Piazza del Popolo 28/29
70011 Alberobello
T: +39 080 432 4082
www.miseriaenobiltaweb.it

Opening hours: 07.00–02.00
Closed: Mon
Holidays: None
Covers: 50 inside; 40 outside
    (with outside heaters in the
    winter)

You can sometimes have too much of a good thing. Take conical roofs. Once you've wandered around Alberobello, you'll have seen enough *trulli* to last a lifetime. Luckily the Palazzo dei Conti di Conversano, in a prime position on the Piazza del Popolo, is an altogether different architectural proposition.

Originally an aristocratic home, it had been abandoned and left to decline for over 30 years when Franco Lacatena happened upon it in 2004. It took him five months to refurbish it, but he did so in style. He opened it as Miseriaenobiltà in March 2005 and in no time at all it became the venue of choice for the locals.

Franco chose the name — the title of an old film — because he liked the reference to the historic poverty, *miseria*, of Alberobello and the nobility of the building. He has respected that nobility. The vaulted ceiling is still a focal point and the modernity, although striking, is sympathetic to the centuries-old stonework.

There is, however, more than a nod to fashion in the form of the inventive interior and the huge MTV screen, not to mention the young and beautiful, who hang out at the bar and adorn the terrace. But this place is as much about food as fashion, as you'll find not only in the bar but in the calmer surroundings of the downstairs dining room.

Franco only serves hams that are DOP (*Denominazione di Origine Protetta,* the Italian equivalent of Protected Designation of Origin). The cheese selection is great too. If you're in the mood for something more adventurous, Nico the chef produces a large selection of appealing, main course salads: rocket and seafood, fennel, gorgonzola and walnuts or mozzarella, tomato, sweetcorn and olives. There's a daily selection of pastas too, and the steak — *tagliata di Angus* — is particularly popular with the locals. As Franco explains: "They eat sausages at home, so they want something different when they go out."

This may be a tourist town but Miseriaenobiltà is clearly not a tourist trap. Franco believes that if there is a strong, local clientele, then the visitors will come for the right reasons. Thus the food is sourced and presented with enthusiasm and care, as is the wine — inevitably, given that Franco is a sommelier. There are about 150 different wines on his list, from Puglia and well beyond. And every day there's a choice of three whites and three reds by the glass. Or if you're in the mood for something more exotic turn up for Franco's cocktails; he's won mixing awards. There's even a happy hour from Thursday to Saturday.

If your preferred time of day is the morning, however, Franco can offer you an American buffet breakfast, albeit with an Italian flavour. Enjoy your fruit, cereals, pastries and coffees at your own pace under a parasol overlooking the Piazza. It's a delightful way to acquire some sustenance before braving the *trulli* crowds.

This is, you will soon realise, far from your archetypal Alberobello restaurant. But it is very much part of Alberobello and Franco is proud of the fact. He had gained valuable experience running a restaurant in the fashionable ski resort of Cortina d'Ampezzo in the Dolomites. But as lovely as he found the Veneto, the pull back home was strong. He is delighted to be part of the Alberobello community. Realising that there was nowhere in town for temporary art displays, he has set aside a wall as an exhibition space for local artists.

But the indoor exhibition isn't the only visual entertainment. There's a fair amount of theatre in the Piazza too. Get yourself a seat on the restaurant terrace and watch a bit of it. Italian life from cradle to grave is on view: parents showing off babies, children running and playing, pre-teens practising their flirting skills (while teenagers show how it should be done), women (and men) showing off their outfits and jewellery, pensioners relaxing and gossiping on the benches. The scene is compelling, bordering on the addictive.

As is dining, drinking or just hanging out at Miseriaenobiltà. Bar, restaurant, art gallery and more: a place that mixes style with substance, but without compromising either. And the perfect refuge from the *trulli* crowds — just in case you need one, of course.

Assortimento di Verdure Grigliate con Stracchino Fresco Profumato alla Menta
Grilled Vegetables with Fresh Cheese and Mint

Franco and his chefs have a wide choice of local vegetables readily available, and throughout the year come up with various ways of serving them when at their best.

SERVES 1

Aubergine, 6 long slices
1/2 yellow pepper
30g fresh Pugliese cheese,
  such as Stracchino
2 cherry tomatoes, halved

Mint leaves, chopped
Parsley, chopped
Salt and pepper
Extra virgin olive oil

Grill the aubergine slices, season and leave to cool. Grill the pepper (to add flavour) so that it remains crunchy and keeps its skin. Then chop it into medium-sized pieces and pile in the centre of the serving plate. Arrange the aubergine slices around the edge and place round shapes of the cheese on these. Place the tomato halves between the aubergine slices and sprinkle over the mint and parsley. Season and dress with the olive oil.

Wine suggestion: White — "Sedna" Salento IGT, Tenute Rubino (Malvasia Bianca)

Insalata Tropicale con Ananas, Fragole, Cocco e Gamberetti
Tropical Salad with Pineapple, Strawberries, Coconut and Prawns

An unusual salad that is popular with Franco's diners on hot summer days.

SERVES 1

50g mild-flavoured green leaves
20g radicchio
20g pineapple
20g strawberries
25g coconut
30g prawns, cooked and shelled

Extra virgin olive oil
Balsamic vinegar
Salt and pepper

Chop the leaves and radicchio into bite-sized pieces and place on a dish. Cut the fruit into pieces and arrange on the leaves, in the order in which they are listed. Finally, place the prawns on top.

Serve with a dressing of oil, vinegar and seasoning to taste.

Wine suggestion: White — Locorotondo DOC, Albea (Verdeca, Bianco d'Alessano, Fiano)

Andria

Andria is approximately 18km from the extraordinary Castel del Monte, an enormous octagonal stone castle, and a majestic example of Swabian architecture atop a lonely peak of the Murge. The city of Andria itself has its own charms: a cathedral, fascinating churches such as San Francesco, San Domenico and Sant'Agostino, and a quaint confectionery museum — *Confetteria Mario Mucci* — whose factory has been creating all manner of sweet treats since 1894. Then again you may need a sugar fix after coping with the bustling Andrian *passeggiata* and the local driving.

De la Poste, Locanda
Nicola Montereale and Stefania Nenna

via G Bovio 49
70031 Andria
T: +39 0883 558 655

Opening hours: 13.00–14.30;
  20.00–23.00
Closed: Sun evening and
  Wed
Holidays: Aug (all month)
Covers: 40 inside

The chef and owner of De la Poste, Locanda is chatting to us about cooking and the excellence of the local produce. Suddenly he breaks off. He points to the piano in the corner of the restaurant and smiles, remembering the many customers who have taken to the keyboard after a few grappas and publicly crooned to their partners. So does he ever serenade Stefania, his wife, who heads up the dining room? "Only with my dishes," he laughs.

Welcome to the world of Nicola Montereale and his restaurant, which, as its name suggests, you will find opposite the central post office in Andria. If you can find it, that is. The charming, rustic interior hides behind a chic, smoked glass entrance, which is easy to miss. Try not to, though; you would also be missing elegant, stylish cooking that hints at both local and international influences and that is more than matched by an excellent wine list.

Dining has long been connected with this site, although it was decidedly less sophisticated in the 1500s and 1600s, when people used to leave their horses outside the post office while taking refreshment. Still, it's a link that appeals to Nicola. In fact, links and continuity of all sorts appeal to him, most obviously the link between good food and good wine, which may explain why he took a sommelier course — and why he and Stefania have one of the most highly regarded wine lists in the north of Puglia.

And that's no mean achievement for a place that opened in 1999 with a much more limited choice: two wines and two waters to be precise. De la Poste, Locanda now boasts an extensive range; and local ones tend to be popular with visitors, while the regulars can choose from a broad selection that takes in other regions of Italy as well as international producers.

Apart, obviously, from wonderful food and a fabulous wine list, an essential aspect of running a successful restaurant, says Nicola, is to have a regular dialogue with your clients — and more importantly to listen to what they have to say. And that's where Stefania comes in. Engaging and efficient, she is the perfect embodiment of Nicola's philosophy of restaurant management.

Of course she lets you know what's on offer, but for her it is more than mindless reciting. She offers the sort of support that is vital in a restaurant where the printed menu can only provide a guideline and backdrop to the daily specials — specials that are taken very, very seriously. She has, by the way, an almost freakish recall of what customers have eaten and drunk both on the day and in past visits. Fads, favourites, preferences, prejudices — she remembers them all.

In contrast to Stefania, who is friendly and effusive, Nicola is calm, almost serene, until, that is, you broach the subject of cooking with fish. Then he gets quite animated. Firstly, he says, the fish must not be imported but "*dai nostri mari*" — "from our seas". Then there's the personal dimension he brings to the local produce. He loves experimenting with influences he's acquired from working elsewhere in Italy and with chefs from other countries. The oriental influences of ginger, soya and algae are a current favourite, and raw fish sushi-style.

But always balanced. "I don't do heavy dishes," he says, "but light dishes with vegetables and fresh fish. I link elements from the sea and the earth, but in a way that one doesn't swamp the other." And, he adds, always using fresh, seasonal vegetables. His favourite times of year are spring and autumn, the seasons of change. Fresh produce is abundant at this time, and for him the arrival of different vegetables is a time of renewed excitement.

And speaking of excitement...the thrill of their recent, and long-awaited wedding may be subsiding, but there's now the ongoing renovation of a house in the historic centre of Andria. They've been supervising the revamp for over two years now, and even though there's still a fair way to go, it's clear that it will be stunning when completed.

And after that? Nicola talks diffidently and obliquely about projects he may have planned for the future. Stefania, meanwhile, muses candidly on the possibility of converting the huge cellar in their new home into a restaurant.

It would certainly have a lot to live up to. Nicola may joke about serenading Stefania with his dishes but, better than that, as a duo they have brought food and wine together with style and welcome in — what would you call it? Perfect harmony, perhaps?

Clockwise from top left:
The restaurant piano, used for occasional public crooning.

Nicola's Aubergine and Roast Pepper Terrine.

Stefania and Nicola outside De la Poste, Locanda.

Orecchiette con Pomodorini, Rucola e Ricotta Dura di Andria
Orecchiette with Cherry Tomatoes, Rocket and Ricotta from Andria

A simple but delicious pasta that gives Nicola the opportunity to use local produce.

SERVES 6

2kg cherry tomatoes, quartered
Extra virgin olive oil, garlic and salt
  to taste
500g orecchiette, or other fresh
  pasta if not readily available

2 bunches rocket, washed, and
  if large leaves, halved/chopped
150g hard ricotta from Andria,
  or matured hard cheese

Cook the tomatoes with the oil, garlic and salt for 5 minutes. In a separate pan, cook the orecchiette for a few minutes and just before they reach al dente, mix in with the tomatoes (where they will continue cooking). Keep a few attractive rocket leaves to one side for garnish, and add the rest to wilt. Serve immediately with shavings of hard ricotta and the saved rocket leaves.

Wine suggestion: White — "Rampone", Valle d'Itria IGT, I Pastini
(Fiano Minutolo)

Fiori di Zucchini Farciti con Calamari Scottati

Stuffed Courgette Flowers with Sautéed Squid

Nicola often serves this with large prawns, but squid is an option for days when the prawns aren't up to his standards.

SERVES 10

300g of sea bass, cleaned, filleted
  and chopped
5 basil leaves
50cl fresh cream
1 large egg white
Salt and pepper to taste
20 fresh courgette flowers
20 thin slices courgette

For the sauce:
1 leek, chopped
1 white onion, chopped

500g carrots, peeled and sliced
Extra virgin olive oil
Vegetable stock as necessary

For the squid:
10 medium squid, cleaned and
  quartered
Extra virgin olive oil
1 garlic clove, peeled and left whole
  to flavour the oil
Thyme

Prepare a stuffing by blending the chopped sea bass with the basil leaves, the cream, the egg white, salt and pepper. Blitz in a blender. Stuff the courgette flowers, and wrap a thin slice of courgette around each flower to keep everything closed and in place. Leave to rest for about an hour in the fridge, so that the stuffing settles in the shape of the flower. In the meantime prepare the carrot sauce by gently frying the leek, onion and carrots in olive oil. Finally add the vegetable stock, and leave to simmer for a while. Liquidise everything, to give a creamy sauce.

Bake the stuffed flowers in a 180°C oven for about 5 minutes. While the flowers are cooking, sauté the squid in the olive oil with the garlic and thyme, using a non-stick frying pan.

Serve 2 flowers per person, laying them carefully on a spoon of carrot sauce with the sautéed squid on the side.

Wine suggestion: White — "Marese", Castel del Monte DOC, Rivera (Bombino Bianco)

Antichi Sapori   Pietro Zito

Piazza S. Isidoro 10
Montegrosso, Andria
T: +39 0883 569 529
www.antichisapori.biz

Opening hours: 12.30–14.30;
 20.00–22.00
 (Reservations essential)
Closed: Sat evening and Sun
Holidays: Easter, Jul (20 days),
 few days either side of 15 Aug,
 Christmas (one week).
Covers: 35

In 1998, there was trouble in the village of Montegrosso. Pietro Zito's restaurant was vandalised. He decided to close. The villagers disagreed. He had to continue, they said, and they would help him. People worked through the night to repair the damage and get the restaurant back on its feet again. That is at least some measure of what Antichi Sapori and Pietro Zito mean to Montegrosso.

Pietro is a gifted cook, but he doesn't claim his passion to be food and cooking. His enthusiasm, he says, is for "agriculture, nature and the earth". The *territorio* informs everything that he does. He goes on to say, however, that his real qualification is "being born here – a farmer".

This feeling for the land wasn't fashionable during Pietro's early years in the business. "Fifteen years ago, restaurants in Puglia were very different," he says. "Restaurateurs didn't believe in their own *territorio*. When we went out to eat we ate salmon and béchamel and those sorts of combinations. If you ate food from your *territorio* you were transported to the past, and that meant poverty."

But Pietro didn't see it that way. His mother made simple food based on local vegetables, pulses and homemade pastas. It was delicious. That was good enough for him. So when, with family help, he opened his osteria a decade and a half ago, he put their money where his heart was and gambled that the locals would feel the same way about well prepared home cooking. Antichi Sapori has been full every day since.

And the formula hasn't changed. Thus, unlike many restaurateurs who go to markets, Pietro goes directly to the neighbouring farmers. "*Il mio supermercato é la campagna*. The countryside is my supermarket," he says. In keeping with this, and the simplicity of his traditional dishes, he barely tweaks them. "I don't want to upset traditional, proven combinations because if I do that I'll lose my roots," he explains.

One consequence of his extraordinary success has been the regeneration of the village of Montegrosso. Younger people are returning, and the residents even help with vegetable harvests and jam-making. Pietro likes the fact that inadvertently he's created a community of like-minded souls whose feet are firmly rooted in agriculture.

And meeting his father, Francesco, it's clear that the apple didn't fall far from the tree. Francesco, a quiet, charming man, not only played a major part in revamping Antichi Sapori but goes out every morning to forage for wild plants on the Murge. For all his mildness, he's fierce in his criticism of what is happening to one of the most valued wild spaces in Puglia. "It's wrong that people are cultivating here," he says. "It should all be left wild. Some days I have to cover 20 kilometres to gather what I used to in one. Plants we ate raw when I was a child now have to be cooked, and their intense flavour is lost. We're losing nature." He explains that, being from the country, he doesn't wash the fruit. "It tastes so much better straight from where it's grown to your mouth. If you buy it from a shop, you don't know how many hands have touched it and every time produce is touched, it loses some of its taste."

Pietro Zito in Antichi Sapori

Not if his son has anything to do with it, it doesn't. And it's not just the quality of his food but the quality of his life that Pietro treasures. Hence the astonishing, many said suicidal, decision to close during the big-taking sittings of Saturday evening and Sunday lunchtime. "It was a life choice," he says simply. "This is hard work and, if you don't draw a line and enforce a limit, you'd collapse." The same thinking dictated Pietro's decision to downsize the restaurant from 60 to 35 covers in 2005. In any case, the higher the number of customers, the less time he had to check on the quality/price relationship of what he serves. And that matters to him.

As does the supply of decent vegetables, which is why he closes Antichi Sapori for most of July and has a holiday. There's also the small matter of the fierce summer heat, so in August he and the team sometimes cater at a nearby organic *masseria*, Lama di Luna, for dinner service only.

At such times the work routine changes somewhat: the beach in the morning, and then a late start to work in the evening when it's cooling down. Plus of course the wonderful view from the Lama di Luna. "The towns are lit up and the trees look like velvet," Pietro sighs.

Whenever he goes away for a while, the Montegrosso inhabitants are delighted when he and his team returns. As one of them says: "It's very unhappy here when they're away. We really miss them. It's great when everyone's back." And when Pietro returns, so too do his favourite vegetables as nearby farmers bring him their produce: different herbs, mushrooms, *lampascioni*, *chicorietta*, wild onions. Autumn and winter clearly inspire him. The restaurant too comes into its own as the nights shorten and it turns into a cosy retreat from the colder seasons.

A retreat that, thanks to Pietro's desire to open people's minds to simple food and cooking, even extends to the kitchen. Before the restaurant was redecorated and sized down, there was a sign saying 'It's not forbidden to enter the kitchen' and patrons were encouraged to walk in and start chatting amid the saucepans. When the local health and safety authorities insisted that this be removed, Pietro started making plans to encourage his cooks to serve their dishes and present their work — bringing the kitchen to your table, if you like.

As if such a performance, on top of coping with a constantly full house at both lunch and dinner, were not enough, Pietro is looking forward to other challenges. Feeling that the *territorio* has given him so much he wants to return the favour. He's keen to teach schoolchildren about the joys of the countryside — or, as he puts it: "*Oltre ai cellulari ci sono i pomodori*. Apart from mobiles there are also tomatoes." He's also increasingly asked to welcome groups of disadvantaged youngsters, so that they can get involved in the wonders of growing, and the

rewards of eating your own produce. In October 2007, a group from London arrived for this life-enhancing experience. And he's developing a vegetable garden with two retired people from the village. Diners at the restaurant will be able to pick vegetables and take them to the restaurant to be cooked or enjoy a dish at the restaurant and then go to collect the raw ingredients from the garden on the way home.

Pietro clearly loves the idea of his dishes both telling a story and giving, as he puts it, that emotion to the table, "*è questo il mio futuro: dare queste emozioni al tavolo*". A touch ambitious? Perhaps not from someone who is able to galvanise a kitchen team to work brilliantly every day. And to mobilise an entire village.

Above left: A rustic corner of Antichi Sapori.

Above: Francesco, Pietro's father, is convinced that fresh produce tastes much better, the fewer hands that have touched it.

Acqua e Sale
"Water and Salt"

This is an old dish of poor farming communities, using up stale bread by soaking in water and salt, hence the name. Pietro, of course, serves his version with freshly picked vegetables from nearby fields.

SERVES 4

10 cherry tomatoes, halved
1/2 clove garlic, finely chopped
1 small red onion, halved and thinly sliced
1/2 cucumber, peeled, halved lengthwise and thinly sliced
Sea salt and pepper

Parsley, chopped
Oregano
Extra virgin olive oil, a generous amount
1/2 glass water
300g old dry bread, cut into small cubes

In a large bowl, put the tomatoes, garlic, onion, cucumber, salt, pepper, parsley, oregano and abundant oil. Mix well. Separately, sprinkle the water over the bread and then mix the bread with the vegetables, so that it is covered in oil.

As soon as the bread starts to soften, serve. Note that the bread should retain some of its crunch, so don't prepare too long before serving.

Wine suggestion: Rosé — Castel del Monte DOC, Giancarlo Ceci (Bombino Nero)

Pancotto con Rucola
Pancotto with Rocket

Pancotto, or "cooked bread", is usually a type of soup. Pietro drains this version so that it is served with only the liquid that the bread has absorbed. This is made by local cooks with whatever vegetables are available and is popular in winter with cime di rape. The base, however, is always bread, water and oil. Bear in mind that the rocket used here is quite a thick and tough strain; if you only have smaller and thinner leaves available, you will need to adjust the timing, and scarcely blanch them.

SERVES 4

1 head garlic, cloves separated
  and peeled
1 chilli
Sea salt
Bay leaf
100cl water

100g rocket leaves, washed
12 cherry tomatoes, quartered
400g hard, stale bread, thickly sliced
  and halved
100cl extra virgin olive oil

Put the garlic, chilli, salt and bay leaf in the water, and bring to the boil. Once boiling, add the rocket leaves and, after a couple of minutes or as soon as cooked, add the tomatoes and bread. Keep an eye on this as timing will depend on the type and staleness of the bread being used; take the pan off the heat and remove everything from the water with a slotted spoon when the bread has softened but before it disintegrates.

Discard the bay leaf, chilli and water. Distribute everything else equally between the serving plates and garnish liberally with olive oil to taste.

Wine suggestion: Red — "Parco Marano" Castel del Monte DOC, Giancarlo Ceci (Uva di Troia)

Bari

Bari is the capital of Puglia — and it feels like it. With its broad boulevards, big-name shops, smartly attired business people and a labyrinthine Old Town, it has wide-ranging appeal. But if that doesn't work for you, try the waterfront, and a walk along the high city wall. When Bari's football team was in Serie B, and nearby Lecce in Serie A, the Baresi would console themselves by proclaiming "our stadium is much better", singing the virtues of Stadio San Nicola designed by the world-famous architect Renzo Piano. Both teams are now in Serie B so architecture isn't the only topic of banter on the terraces. But it's still a better stadium.

Il Pane e le Rose
Giovanni Attoma and Emanuele Sciannimanico

via Roberto da Bari 128
70121 Bari
T: +39 080 523 9176

Opening hours: 12.30–15.00;
  18.30–01.00 (or later)
Closed: Sun (Jun–Jul);
  Sun lunchtime only
  (Sept–May)
Holidays: Aug (all month)
Covers: 25

Spanish ham, Breton oysters and Japanese sashimi — in the centre of Puglia's capital? For those of us who assumed that all good restaurants in Italy only served seasonal food from their *territorio*, Il Pane e le Rose is something of a surprise.

Emanuele Sciannimanico, the co-owner, explains. "Bari is a port so there is an open mentality here," he says. "The Baresi are usually ready to embrace things from outside and abroad because culturally they are very receptive."

There is, of course, a little more to it than that. Emanuele and his business partner Giovanni Attoma got to know each other when Emanuele worked in a Pugliese restaurant and Giovanni was working in a well-known *birreria* nearby. On some free evenings they would visit each other's places and chat — chat about wanting to dine in a way that wasn't possible in Bari, and to drink wines not just from Puglia but from other regions, other countries — even other continents. Nobody else was offering that so "together we decided to do something different".

It was an idea out of left field — with a name to match. "The reference to German revolutionary Rosa Luxembourg's creed of both bread for sustenance and roses for a quality of life suits our place very well," says Emanuele. "We don't only provide food and drink, but cultural information too, as well as the chance to chat, discuss and make friends with like-minded people."

They were adamant that the market was there; it was simply a case of finding it. And find it they did. Il Pane e le Rose attracts a large number of educated professionals, the culturally aware, the well travelled. "When they're abroad working or studying they gravitate towards places like ours — and then want to find something similar when they return," says Emanuele.

So...an erudite and interesting bunch savouring light platters of cold hams, cheeses and salads and an out-of-the-ordinary wine list, you might think. And you might be right. But that doesn't mean that Il Pane e le Rose is stuffy or exclusive.

There's a relaxed atmosphere enhanced by music, generally oriented towards lounge jazz. There's also a conscious effort to make those who are less than used to the formalities of dining, especially the young, feel at ease. "We serve wine as we would any other drink, without going on about perfumes and all the rest of it," says Emanuele. Don't think they're frivolous about wine, though. If you want to know about grapes and vineyards you'll find them more than happy to educate you. As Emanuele puts it: "Giving advice is the best part of my job. If you're introducing new things to people you have to encourage a dialogue. We are growing ourselves, and consequently we offer different things to our public. And so they are growing along with us".

And that applies to food as well as wine. "Because our clients are regular and come three, maybe four times a week, they are ready to try different things. That's why we offered Japanese dishes: it's something new."

Discovering those new dishes is a part of the job they find especially satisfying. It even extends to their time off, although here their tastes diverge. Giovanni

Above left: Regular lunchtime diners relaxing.

Above: Giovanni Attoma explaining new additions to the menu.

explains: "It's a generational thing. I'm 55 and my generation had France as a reference point." Hence he holidays in France and Belgium, where he also seeks out chocolate for Il Pane e le Rose. Emanuele, meanwhile, seeks out the culinary delights of Australia, New Zealand, South Africa, Ireland or Britain.

The influence of their travels even extends to the décor. They wanted, as Emanuele puts it, "to break up the monotony of the 'classic': the arches, the vaults, wooden tables, wicker chairs. It seemed already done — and oppressive, because everything is the same." They both travelled around major European centres and studied the best design journals, although ironically they got the results they wanted much closer to home.

The modern décor is mainly the work — and the first commission — of a young architectural student, although the use of plexiglass tables featuring the establishment's logo was Emanuele's and Giovanni's idea. And the design of the logo? That came from a communications agency. As you'd expect. After all, the owners do see the place as a modern form of communication.

It was soon obvious that the clean interior lent itself to the display of artwork, except that they couldn't decide what to display. Much discussion between themselves and their clients later and up went a selection of photographs. There has been a constantly changing photographic exhibition ever since, the only common theme being that, to date, all the photographers either hail from or live in Bari. And very fashionable they are too, but then Emanuele believes that Bari culturally and commercially has a lot more in common with trendsetters in the north than with the rest of the south. "We look more closely at Milano that we do at Napoli or Palermo," he explains.

As you'll have guessed by now, Giovanni and Emanuele's offering is a bit different. An establishment firmly rooted in Bari and its community that serves food and wine from everywhere else. A cultural conduit but also a place just to drink, eat and relax. Not quite a restaurant but not quite a wine bar either.

That, however, is something they have tried to clarify. They settled for the Italian, *vineria* "because we didn't want to come down on the side of the Anglophile with wine bar nor that of the Francophile with *bar à vins*".

Il Pane e le Rose may not be easy to define, but the regulars clearly get it. Perhaps that's why, though Emanuele and Giovanni offer little specifically Pugliese, the result is pure Barese.

Clockwise from left:
The modern interior lends itself to the constantly changing photographic exhibition.

Emanuele Sciannimanico

The small bar area adds to the relaxed atmosphere.

Insalata Caprese Caprese Salad

*Emanuele and Giovanni always use Mozzarella di Latte di Podolica, mozzarella
from Podolica cows made by the Caseificio Masi, but you can obviously substitute
whatever good fior di latte or mozzarella you can find. If you order this at Il Pane e le
Rose, you'll always be served Pachino tomatoes (from Sicily) which are particularly
full of flavour, and extra virgin olive oil DOP Terra di Bari.*

SERVES 1

1 large mozzarella, 250g
1 large tomato, sliced
Extra virgin olive oil

Dried oregano
Basil leaves

Cut slices almost all the way through the mozzarella, and place slices of tomato
in them. Drizzle over the oil, and sprinkle over the oregano and serve garnished
with the basil leaves.

**Wine suggestion: Sparkling — Franciacorta DOCG Brut, Contadi Castaldi
(Chardonnay, Pinot Bianco, Pinot Nero)**

Pera Caramellata al Vino Primitivo Pears in Red Wine

The taste contrast between the sweetness of the pear in wine with the salty cheese is delicious. Giovanni opts to serve this deep red dish on a bright yellow plate for dramatic effect.

SERVES 1

250cl Primitivo wine, or a full-bodied 14° red wine
250g caster sugar
2 cinnamon sticks
A few cloves

Star anise
A few black pepper grains
1 ripe Abate pear, peeled
To serve: mature Pugliese Pecorino, or similar

Bring the wine, sugar, cinnamon, cloves, star anise and pepper to the boil. Place the pear gently in the pan for 5 minutes on a vigorous simmer. Remove the pear, strain the wine and then reduce until thick.

Serve the pear with small pieces of the cheese, and with the reduced wine to taste.

Wine suggestion: Dessert Red — "Primo Amore" Primitivo di Manduria DOC Dolce Naturale, Pervini (Primitivo)

PerBacco Beppe Schino

via Abbrescia 99
70121 Bari
T: +39 080 558 0179

Opening hours: Mon–Fri
 13.00–15.00; 20.00–24.00;
 Sat open only for dinner
Closed: Sat lunch and
 all day Sun
Holidays: Jul and Aug
 (all month)
Covers: 36

PerBacco? Per Bacco! By Jove! according to the dictionary. By Bacchus! literally and according to Beppe Schino. He wanted a name for his restaurant that celebrated wine. The name of the Greek god of the grape seemed to fit the bill — with an exclamatory flourish.

And, by Bacchus, Beppe has a right to celebrate. After a long period of study and many years as a practising architect his full-time job now involves pursuing his love of "food, wine and the joys of sitting at a table with friends".

The radical career change was inspired, if that's the word, by boredom: he was finding restaurants in Bari increasingly predictable. So too, he soon realised from family discussions, was his wife's sister. Not only that, but with a background that included the Académie des Beaux-Arts, she also had ideas about how a restaurant should look. Realising that they were on the same wavelength, they decided to create a restaurant. It would be relaxed and casual, it would make diners feel very much at home, but, most important, it would offer a choice of dishes that steered well clear of the expected.

Like so many Italians, Beppe's love of food and cooking was inspired by a mother who encouraged her three eldest sons to take an interest in the kitchen — not least to prevent them wrecking the house. Even now she's a constant influence on the menu through the *Torta della Nonna*, an utterly delicious dessert that she — and only she — makes for the restaurant.

All of which doesn't mean that Beppe has lost his passion for architecture. He feels that he has simply taken his creativity in another direction. In fact he believes there are many ways in which both cooking and architecture meet, not least aesthetically.

Clockwise from top left:
PerBacco is relaxed and casual.

Mirko, aka DJ Argento, is the chef at PerBacco.

Beppe Schino, who left architecture to pursue his love of "food, wine and the joys of sitting at a table with friends."

Fresh, seasonal fruit is a popular dessert.

Above left: The amusing kitchen door was painted by Beppe's sister-in-law.

Above: Cooking in progress in the PerBacco kitchen.

And he doesn't bow or scrape to custom either. "I believe that traditions need to be rejuvenated and replenished," he says. "They have to be allowed to evolve, otherwise they become chains that prevent us from moving."

Aesthetics? Evolution? What flights of fancy populate the PerBacco menu? Don't worry; you're in safe hands. Start off with bread from Altamura, which is among the best in Italy. Or you could try a salad — maybe a warm one with goat's cheese and walnuts. *Fricelli*, a fresh pasta prepared with smoked fish, aubergines and fillets of dried tomatoes, is a favourite of the regulars. There's also a fine assortment of cheeses. To finish, fresh, seasonal fruit can be served with added liqueur and cream. Nothing outlandish, then, but certainly not commonplace.

And that goes for the chef too. Beppe is aided in the kitchen at present by the wacky Mirko, known to young local party animals as DJ Argento, a passionate James Brown fan. "I like it funky funky!" he exclaims. Beppe keeps Mirko away from the in-house sound system, however, and channels his exuberance into some fine dishes.

And the wine? This is PerBacco after all. Thirty per cent of the wines at Per-Bacco are from Puglia, but Beppe also features wines from other regions of Italy and an international selection that encompasses France, Australia, New Zealand, America, Hungary, Austria…"something from everywhere".

That sense of adventure, he feels, sums up his region. "Bari doesn't have a strong gastronomic culture and it hasn't stagnated in culinary customs," he says. It's a philosophy he espouses, naturally, but there's a modest irony in his success: by refusing to follow fashion and insisting on creating his own style, he's built up a loyal clientele of like-minded people.

But it hasn't been easy. Six years after they set up PerBacco, and aged only 40, his sister-in-law Antonella died. She lives on in her paintings and drawings: you can see them on the walls and kitchen door and by the entrance. Beppe suddenly had to decide whether to carry on alone. That he has succeeded is, he says, in large part thanks to the sacrifices of his wife and family. But his own hard work has a lot to do with it.

Not that he's complaining. Running a restaurant was his dream and, as he says, "dreams keep you young. If you don't have at least one a day, you'll age too quickly." Per Bacco!

The entrance hallway.

Fricelli con Pesce Spada Affumicato, Melanzane e Filetti di Pomodori Secchi
Fricelli with Smoked Swordfish, Aubergines and Sun Dried Tomatoes

This is a favourite of many of Beppe's regulars. He explains that "as it is a dish vaguely based on Sicilian flavours", one of his wine suggestions is a Sicilian white; the other wine recommendation is a rosé as "in Puglia there is a tradition of accompanying fish dishes with rosato."

SERVES 4

1 small round aubergine, approx 200g, peeled (the round ones are less bitter than the long)
Extra virgin olive oil
100g smoked swordfish, in one piece
1 garlic clove, peeled
1/2 glass dry white wine
Salt and white pepper to taste

4/5 sun dried tomatoes, cut into strips
320g fresh fricelli (typical Salentine pasta) or another fresh pasta eg cavatelli
Handful fresh parsley, chopped
A few additional slices of swordfish for garnish

Cut the aubergine into slices of about ½ cm and then into strips. Fry them quickly with a little extra virgin olive oil, and then leave on a gentle heat for about 5 minutes until cooked. Put to one side.

Slice the swordfish quite thinly, then chop and cook gently in a deep frying pan with a little extra virgin olive oil and a whole garlic clove. When the swordfish is sautéed, add the wine to the pan and leave on a moderate heat until it has evaporated. Add seasoning to taste, the tomatoes and the aubergine. It is ready when you can no longer smell the wine, ie the taste remains but the perfume disappears. Remove the garlic.

Meanwhile, cook the pasta in abundant salted water. When barely cooked, mix the pasta with the sauce and sauté briefly in the pan, adding the chopped parsley.

Serve with a parsley garnish and thin slices of raw swordfish.

Wine suggestion: Rosé — Castel del Monte DOC, Giancarlo Ceci (Bombino Nero) or White — "Bizir" Sicilia IGT, Ajello (Chardonnay, Grillo, Insolia)

Bavarese alle Fragole Strawberry Bavarois

One of Beppe's fruit-based desserts for those who want something a bit more self-indulgent than raw and natural seasonal fruit.

SERVES 4

300g strawberries, washed, and a few reserved for garnish
100ml milk
100g sugar

2 sheets gelatine
100ml fresh cream
Fresh mint to garnish

Liquidise the strawberries and milk and warm up in a saucepan on a gentle heat. Add the sugar and stir until dissolved. In the meantime, soften the gelatine in cold water. Off the heat, dissolve the gelatine into the strawberry mixture. Leave to cool.

Whip the cream, saving some for decoration if wished. Add to the strawberry mixture and mix thoroughly.

Pour into individual serving moulds and leave in the fridge for 2–3 hours. To serve, remove from the moulds and decorate with cut strawberries, cream and fresh mint.

Wine suggestion: Dessert Red — "Paesano" Salento IGT, Cantine Due Palme (Aleatico) or, Dessert White — "Le Ricordanze" Salento IGT Passito, Cosimo Taurino (Semillon, Riesling)

Brindisi

The port of Brindisi has a fair amount of history behind it. There's a
column denoting the end of the Via Appia, *Colonne Terminali della Via
Appia* or the *Monumento al Marinaio d'Italia*, the Monument to the
Italian Sailor (on the opposite bank). It has always been a gateway to the
east and in recent times to Greece (even the road signs indicate *Grecia*).
However, if you're anticipating a faded port, you may be pleasantly
surprised: relaxed pedestrianised areas with interesting shops and charming
caffès along the waterfront's main road make a visit to Brindisi more
varied than many people would imagine.

Trattoria Pantagruele Armando Brenda

via Salita di Ripalta 1/3
72100 Brindisi
T: +39 0831 560 605

Opening hours: 12.30–14.30;
  19.30–23.00
Closed: Sat lunchtime and all
  day Sun
Holidays: 15 days in Aug
Covers: 45 inside; 25 outside

Armando Brenda may seem a bit outspoken. He's certainly forthright, especially when he rants about the speed of modern life. "I'm against technological advances if all we get is the ability to do 32 hours' work in eight hours," he says. He refuses to own a mobile phone: if he can't be contacted that's his lookout, he says. In any case, "I'm the normal one — it's the rest of you who aren't."

Blunt? Don't believe it for a moment. When you're his guest, you feel special. Take the many regulars, for example: they're a big-hearted lot but a little demanding. One wants the tomato salad, but only if the tomatoes are at their peak of ripeness. Another wants the *gamberoni* but only if they are "*freschisimmi*". Some want the excellent fish that Armando buys twice a day from Brindisi market; others insist on the delicious meats. Assurances are given and food delivered. Not long after that the cleaned plates go back to the kitchen — with copious compliments to the chef. Armando looks after all his regulars.

And he is equally solicitous of the occasional visitors. There is usually a fair smattering of lone diners at Pantagruele, most of them in Brindisi on business. It's not just the food that tempts them back when they visit; it's the relaxed atmosphere. Armando, when he isn't greeting everybody and serving every table at least once, will stop by for a chat or, if that's not what's wanted, leave the diner alone to reflect, read or people watch.

Armando has been running Pantagruele on the via Salita di Ripalta, just a few steps from the Brindisi waterfront, since 1988. He originally had a restaurant round the corner, albeit with just four tables. Starting small was no bad thing, he says, as "I learnt that running a restaurant is about so much more than putting food on tables. To do it well, excellent teamwork is essential." His staff, eager to help, are the embodiment of this philosophy.

When originally setting up Pantagruele, his intention was to create a place where people felt at home — hence the personal touches. The paintings and photos on the walls "have to mean something to me. They have to evoke emotion. By that I mean that they move me, and I hope that they move my diners as well." They came, unsurprisingly from his home to this, his...well, second home, you might say. Or possibly his first given the amount of time he spends there, although this is a cultural requirement, apparently. "There are big differences between the north and the south of Italy," Armando explains. "Here in the south, we'd never sit down to dinner at 7.30; it's still too hot and makes no sense. That's why we're still eating at midnight and 1am."

Believe it or not, he does have a life outside his restaurant. He enjoys gardening; all the restaurant vases are filled with his flowers. He also loves reading, particularly the classics. In fact the restaurant's name comes from the works of Rabelais: Pantagruele was the giant Gargantua's son who had a huge appetite. His real love, however, aside from his family, is his boat.

Armando is proud of being Brindisino and has never wanted to leave; that's partly down to his love of the sea. You can see a big, framed picture of his boat in the first room of the restaurant. It's called *Il Lupo Cattivo* — The Big Bad Wolf —

Above left: Armando Brenda greets everybody and serves every table at least once.

Above: Diners are encouraged to relax and take their time, especially outside in the summer.

or so it seems until you look a bit closer. Armando decided on the name when he bought it but there weren't enough letter 'i's available in time for the launch. It's bad luck to launch a boat without a name so he bought a 'y' instead. It's been Il Lupo Cattyvo ever since. Still, as he says: "Boats often have strange names. Besides, it's better than naming your boat after your wife because then you have the nuisance of changing your boat's name if you change her." He has, incidentally, been married for 35 years. The boat's only been around for 30.

And the restaurant for only 20, but there's a good chance he'll stick with that too. He can barely leave as it is. Certainly if diners are in no rush to go home, that's fine with Armando. His kitchen closes at 10.30pm but he'll continue serving "non-cooked things: cheese, fruit, *digestivi*", until the early hours of the morning.

Why hurry? Sit back for a while at Pantagruele, relax and take things slowly. That seems to be the restaurant's overriding message, although Armando puts it more concisely — of course. "It's a short life," he says. "Stop running and enjoy it."

Above left: Armando buys his excellent fish twice daily from Brindisi market.

Above: The Pantagruele staff work well together and are eager to help.

Maltagliati con Funghi Cardoncelli
Maltagliati with Cardoncelli Mushrooms

*Mushrooms go wonderfully with pasta and here Armando uses maltagliati,
which are "badly cut" — and hence oddly shaped — bits of home-made pasta.*

SERVES 4

For the pasta:
400g type "0" flour
50cl water
1 egg, beaten
Salt

50cl extra virgin olive oil
1 clove garlic, peeled and left whole
100cl white wine

**500g cardoncelli mushrooms,
cleaned and roughly sliced**
Salt and pepper
100g pancetta, cut into julienne strips
**200g tomatoes, skinned, seeded and
diced**
1 sprig marjoram
Chilli pepper to taste
100g goat's cheese, grated

To make the pasta, mix the flour, water, egg and salt together. Work the dough
with your hands until it rolls out thinly and cut roughly into squares or rhombi
of a few centimetres. Leave to rest for 30 minutes at room temperature.

In the meantime, make the mushroom sauce by heating the oil in a
saucepan with the garlic. Add the mushrooms and cook gently before adding
the wine and reducing. Season as required.

Heat a non-stick saucepan, and add the pancetta. As soon as it becomes
crunchy add the mushroom sauce, tomatoes, marjoram, and chilli, and leave
everything to cook.

In plenty of water, cook the pasta and drain. Remove the garlic clove from
the mushroom mixture, and stir in the pasta. Serve with the cheese and a few
leaves of marjoram.

**Wine suggestion: Red — "Selvarossa" Salice Salentino DOC Riserva, Cantine
Due Palme (Negroamaro, Malvasia Nera)**

Gamberi o Scampi "Pantagruele"
"Pantagruele" Langoustine or Shrimp

With fish as fresh as Armando's, minimal interference is necessary, or indeed desired. This is his delicious house speciality, and just right on hot days when something delicious but light is what's wanted.

SERVES 4

800g large prawns (6 per serving)
Salt
100g extra virgin olive oil
Parsley, chopped to taste
Oregano, chopped to taste

1 clove garlic, very finely chopped
1 lemon, quartered for garnish

Boil the shellfish in plenty of salted water for a few minutes. Before draining them, reserve a cup of the cooking liquid.

On a serving platter, arrange the shellfish, and sprinkle over a few drops of the saved water. Finish by adding a stream of oil, some parsley, oregano and garlic. Serve garnished with a wedge of lemon.

Wine suggestion: White — "Bolina" Salento IGT, Calò Rosa del Golfo (Verdeca)

Carovigno

Carovigno is also known as the *Città of Nzegni*. *Nzegni* is one of the more obscure town designations; it's a dialect word signifying flags and banners with religious associations.

However, despite the flag-waving implications, Carovigno is actually an unassuming place: the modest cathedral's address is no. 23 via Cattedrale. In fact if you arrive at lunchtime, you may even wonder if it's inhabited. However, after lunch the townspeople reappear and its veterans fill the benches in the open part of Corso Vittorio Emanuele and chatter away in the presence of Padre Pio, or at least his statue.

Osteria Già Sotto L'Arco
Teresa Galeone Buongiorno and Teodosio Buongiorno

corso Vittorio Emanuele 71
72012 Carovigno
T: +39 0831 996 286
www.giasottolarco.it

Opening hours: 12.30–14.30;
 20.00–23.00
Closed: Mon
Holidays: no set dates
Covers: 35 (including two
 outside on the balcony)

It's 12.30 on a fiercely hot, bright Sunday afternoon. Carovigno is sizzling and the main piazza is full of people seeking shade and caffeine, or trying to squeeze into the overflowing Chiesa del Carmine's confirmation services.

There is, however, a different sort of sanctuary just a few steps above the piazza: Osteria Già Sotto L'Arco. Once a basic eatery and situated on the ground floor beneath the arches, it has been transformed over the last decade by Teodosio Buongiorno and his wife Teresa into an elegant first floor restaurant offering a stunning range of dishes.

The original osteria, established by Teodosio's grandparents, served house wine with simple snacks and fried fish. When his parents took over in 1971 they added uncomplicated dishes such as soups and *orecchiette*. The place was packed out every night. And from the age of 11, Teodosio helped out. However, by his late teens being the next generation of Buongiorno to run the place was a less than appealing idea.

Then he met Teresa on the Carovigno to Brindisi school bus. Like him she wasn't keen on his parents' venture. "Being stuck in a restaurant night after night just didn't interest me," she says.

The young couple agreed that a condition of their marrying was that they would under no circumstances carry on the family business. So Teodosio went into nursing, and Teresa studied accountancy. Then they tried opening a newsagent's. And then a shoe shop. Anything, in fact, to keep out of the restaurant business.

Ironically, throughout this time they were still lending a hand in the osteria. But having full-time jobs and then working evenings in the restaurant was hard going. Add two young children into the mix and it was very stressful. Finally, they

Clockwise from top left :
The entrance to Osteria Già
Sotto L'Arco.

Teodosio, "King of the Dining
Room".

One of Teresa's signature dishes:
Burrata in Pasta Kataifi.

A basic eatery has been
transformed over the last decade
into an elegant restaurant.

decided enough was enough. They would dispense with other distractions and work full time in the osteria.

But they should have seen it coming. Even then, Teresa had moved from assisting at the hob, by making the risottos and dishes that Teodosio's mother couldn't manage, to taking over the kitchen completely. And though she had been horrified by the idea of restaurant work, Teresa had always loved cooking. "My father was a hunter and forager, and when I was young he'd return home with all sorts of goodies, interesting mushrooms for instance, and I'd concoct ways of using them," she says.

And Teodosio, meanwhile, had realised that he loves being in contact with people. Hence their agreement that he is king of the dining room and she is queen of the kitchen. At least that's the theory. As Teodosio does the daily shop, he does have a certain influence on *la cucina*.

Not that Teodosio is a novice. As he tells it: "I began to do the restaurant shopping when I was 18. The first day I returned home with boxes of fruit from the market, only to be told that everything I'd bought was substandard. The next day all agreed that the produce I'd bought was wonderful. But, I'd paid way, way too much. It took me a while but I finally learnt how to do the shopping well."

Teresa has loved cooking since her days as a youngster, concocting ways of using what her father brought home from his hunting and foraging.

Opposite: The setting is beautiful: great care and time has been dedicated to the choice of tables, and chairs, crockery and artwork.

As for Teresa, it's hard to believe that she's had no formal training. Her dishes are full of flavour with a considered balance of textures and colours. From the moment you catch sight of, and smell, fellow diner's plates being served, your mouth will start to water.

So there they were: finally doing jobs they enjoyed in a successful establishment. Successful — just like so many other trattorie. And that was the problem. As Teodosio puts it: "There was no satisfaction in it. People used to come to eat things that they ate at home. We said: 'We will be restaurateurs but we won't do this type of restaurant'."

However, when Teodosio and Teresa decided they wanted to upgrade their parents' simple osteria, it came as a big shock — and not only to their family and friends. In came a long menu and a wine list. Out went the mixed grill and carafe of local red — and with them all the regulars. It took only two days for the restaurant to change from being completely full to completely empty.

But Teodosio and Teresa kept going. They knew they were doing the right thing; it was simply a matter of being able to hang on. And slowly, painfully slowly it sometimes seemed, things turned around. Word of mouth spread from their initial three customers. One, a sales rep, would arrive each week with a large group of clients and push the boat out. Then there was a young girl who worked for the Bishop. Once he'd retired for the night, she'd call to check if she could turn up with a group of friends. "That helped us to pay the electricity bill and do the shopping," Teodosio says.

His parents remained baffled by the changes, but Teodosio's father nevertheless announced one day in April, a few years after the transformation had started, that the family would rally round until the end of September "because summer is an important time". And they did — until September 30, when Teodosio's father stated in passing: "Tomorrow is October 1, so none of us will be here to help."

And sure enough, the next day, a fully booked Saturday no less, no helpers arrived. "There were just the two of us, and we were completely full," says Teodosio. "Can you imagine?" But, he adds: "I learnt a lot from that. We had to be determined. Completely resolute about our decision. If you want to follow a path, there will be obstacles, but you just need to remove them."

And they still feel passionately about the restaurant: what it should serve, how it should look — and even what it should say to its customers. As Teodosio puts it: "The most important aspect of running a restaurant is taste, and taste is not just about the palate. If you enjoy good food, then you'll certainly also enjoy architecture, art, good wine and other fine things." This is why the couple ensure that the setting not only reflects their tastes but complements the food served.

It is undoubtedly a beautiful setting, achieving that difficult mix of formality and relaxation. Designed by an architect friend of the couple, it inhabits its space harmoniously. The flooring reflects the geometry of the room, and great care and time has been dedicated to the choice of everything, from tables and chairs to crockery and artwork. Even finding the right tablecloths took them a year.

Not that either of them sees the work as being done. Osteria Già Sotto L'Arco is constantly evolving — and the diners are enjoying every change. It's a far cry from the early days. In fact, one table here has become perhaps the most sought after dining spot in Puglia.

The single table on the small balcony is a majestic spot. The 'million dollar table' seats two and it's an enchantingly romantic haven above the humdrum comings and goings of the Piazza. If you're lucky enough to be able to book this, you'll doubtless agree with Teodosio's conviction that "it's easier to be explosive. It's much more of a challenge to be calm and tranquil." But then the easy route is never as satisfying.

The "million dollar" table on the balcony which seats only two.

Orecchiette con Cozze e Piselli
Orecchiette with Mussels and Peas

*Teresa feels "blessed to be in a small town surrounded by lots of small farmers".
It helps too that Teodosio has forged excellent relationships with the best local
producers. This means that she receives vegetables within a few hours of them
being picked, which is of course a real benefit as far as peas are concerned.*

SERVES 4

500g shelled peas
Iced water
1 large onion, finely chopped
Extra virgin olive oil
Salt and freshly ground pepper

**600g mussels, carefully cleaned and
    sorted**
1 clove garlic, finely chopped
10cl brandy
**400g orecchiette, or other fresh pasta
    shapes, or gnocchi if preferred**

Boil half the peas for a short time in salted water, drain and cool immediately in
a bowl of iced water. Put in a bowl to one side. In the meantime, sweat the onion
in a pan with some oil, and add the remaining peas. Continue cooking on a high
heat: pour on 2 ladles of hot water and cook for 30 minutes. Check the seasoning
and then put into a blender to obtain a purée.

   Add the cleaned and closed mussels to a wide pan with a drop of oil, put on
a high heat and cover. Once the mussels have opened, remove from the heat and
leave on one side to cool down. Discard any that have not opened. Retain 16 of
the best in their shells for the garnish and shell the others.

   For the sauce, heat some oil and the garlic in a pan and quickly sauté the
mussels. Pour over the brandy and leave to evaporate. Add the pea purée and mix
so that the flavours combine.

   In the meantime, boil the orecchiette in plenty of salted water. Drain when
barely al dente and mix in with the sauce so that they finish cooking. Dish up and
decorate each plate with four of the mussels still in their shells, the previously
reserved peas and a generous grind of pepper.

**Wine suggestion: White — "Teresa Manara", Salento IGT,
Cantele (Chardonnay)**

Torta Meringata con Crema e Fichi Mandorlati
Cream and Almond Fig Meringue Pie

Teresa loves making desserts as "there's so much imagination involved". It's usually easy to spot the regulars at Già Sotto L'Arco: they're the people who have left space for a final sweet treat.

SERVES 4

250g shortcrust pastry	**Meringue:**
200g confectioner's cream	**2 egg whites**
5–6 dried figs stuffed with almonds and soaked in San Marsano liqueur, stalks removed and chopped	**100g icing sugar**

Roll out the pastry, and line a greased baking dish of 22cm diameter to a thickness of about 1cm. Bake blind until the pastry is cooked but is still uniformly pale. Leave to cool. Fill with the cream, and scatter the chopped figs over the top. Beat the egg whites and sugar to a stiff meringue, and put in a piping bag and decoratively cover the tart. Put in a preheated oven at 100°C for 90 minutes. The meringue should be hard, but white.

Leave to cool before serving, and decorate to your own personal taste.

Wine suggestion: Dessert — "Le Briciole" Salento IGT Passito, Azienda Monaci (Chardonnay, Malvasia Bianca)

Ceglie Messapica

A short distance from Ostuni, Ceglie Messapica has far fewer tourists. Its old town is full of bright white houses lining narrow streets and its castle and churches are worth a visit, but it has mainly made a name for itself in recent years as a centre of gastronomy. This is hardly surprising given that agriculture is the largest employer. Should you need to ask for directions, by the way, opt for younger rather than older passers-by unless you're up to speed with the local dialect.

Al Fornello Da Ricci
Antonella Ricci and Vinod Sookar

Contrada Montevicoli
72013 Ceglie Messapica
T: +39 0831 377 104

Opening hours: 12.45–15.30;
  20.00–22.30
Closed: Mon evening and Tues
Holidays: 20 days in Sept
  and 10 days at end of Feb
Covers: 60 inside, or 60 outside

The story so far: girl brought up in solid, Catholic, conservative family with strong culinary grounding broadens her mind at university. She then develops her cooking skills and returns home bringing with her the flair and innovative ideas developed in both her training and travels. Ends up running family restaurant. Now try guessing the next chapter.

But first ask anyone in the know to recommend a long-established, well-regarded place to eat in Puglia. Chances are they'll send you to Al Fornello da Ricci on the outskirts of Ceglie Messapica. It was set up by Antonella Ricci's grandmother in 1967 and then handed over to her mother, Dora. Antonella "born in the kitchen", according to Dora, was next in line. "I always intended to be a cook," she says.

So far, so straightforward. However, committed though Antonella was to becoming a chef and continuing the family business, she took some time out to get an economics degree from the University of Lecce. She still came home every weekend to help out, though, and she cooked a bit in the student house she shared with four other girls. Actually, she cooked a lot. Every week the question on campus was "when is Antonella cooking?" When the answer was "today", the house got a bit crowded.

Her studies went well, she graduated with little fuss and then she turned her attention, as she had always planned, back to cooking. It was then that she got her first major break when she was one of ten children of Italian restaurateurs to win a competition. The prize was a dream come true for Antonella: the chance to study at the Institut Paul Bocuse at Ecully, near Lyon and benefit from work experience with one of the world's most famous chefs. "I was very excited," she says. "I

The beautiful, fragrant and colourful garden is a popular spot to dine in the summer.

knew lots, everything about Pugliese cooking — it was in my blood. But I knew there was so much more, and the rest I had to learn."

And learn she did. Bocuse and the French experience were a seminal influence and not only expanded but consolidated what she had learned since her first time in the kitchen. She returned to Ceglie Messapica, not only more assured and accomplished, but with even greater motivation.

All was not well, however. Her then boyfriend had no interest in her chosen profession and gave her a choice: it was either him or cooking. Bad move. "I chose cooking, and told him to go," says Antonella. But the experience still left her feeling a bit down.

That's when the phone call came that, as they say in magazines, changed her life. A well-known chef, Igles Corelli, called up to say that he had to back out of a week-long showcase of Pugliese cooking. Could she go in his place? And, by the way, it was in Mauritius.

Antonella accepted the offer; she had been looking for some distraction in any case. She got a lot more than she expected. "Twenty days later I was in a Mauritian kitchen, being introduced to my assistant for the week: Vinod. All I could say was "Grazie!""

They were together constantly. Back then, Vinod didn't even speak Italian so they communicated in French. And then, after only a week, it was over. Antonella was distraught. "When I went to the airport, I was weeping uncontrollably. The PR lady said to me: "You're going home, there's nothing to worry about." And I said: "But I want to stay here!!""

Her mood was rather better when she went to Bari airport a few months later to meet a successful applicant for work placement at the restaurant. "At least that's what we told my parents." The new employee at Al Fornello da Ricci was, inevitably, Vinod. Still, Antonella's parents did find out eventually. "One day," says Vinod, "I sat down with Angelo, Antonella's father, and explained that, although I was here for work experience I also wanted to marry Antonella."

And precisely one year after they met, and with the blessings of both sets of parents, that is exactly what happened — twice: a Catholic wedding in Italy and a Hindu wedding in Mauritius. For the Italian celebration they insisted on the best caterers possible: themselves. "It was completely mad," they admit. But they did it. Just. At 3pm they were still working in the kitchen. At 5pm Antonella was in the church with her bouquet.

Cooking, you will have guessed, is more to them than just a job. Antonella's

Above left: Vinod's *Mattonella* of white chocolate.

Above: The antipasto platter is deservedly popular

cooking in particular is grounded in the traditions of her family and those of the region. That respect for Puglia's traditions and raw materials, combined with her technical ability, has certainly helped her creative process. "Knowledge of these things and how tastes work together have helped me to develop dishes of my own," she says. But her tastes don't start and end in Puglia. She also has a keen eye and enthusiastic curiosity for those of other cultures.

Such as, say, Mauritius, whose cooking is, says Vinod, "born from various ethnic groups. It's beautiful to see cooking evolving and continually growing." The fusion of French, Indian and Chinese that is the basis of much of the island's cooking has even prompted multi-ethnic culinary excursions at Al Fornello da Ricci. "The idea came about because there was a Malaysian girl working in the kitchen, along with a Japanese trainee," says Vinod. "I'm Mauritian and Antonella is Italian so we had a cultural mix raring to go." Trialled the year he arrived, it was a huge success. Word spread and the phone didn't stop ringing with requests for places at the next one. However, you may find it hard to book. "We hold only one a year," says Antonella. "It wouldn't be special if we did it all the time."

Unlike Antonella, Vinod is the first person in his family to become a chef, but he is no less determined than his wife. He learned the fundamentals of his

Antonella always knew that she would end up in the restaurant set up by her grandmother.

trade when he was one of only 30 — out of 400 — to get on a course at his island's hotel school. He's researched techniques in Italy and done gastronomic tours in Spain. And he's still keen to learn. "I'd like to make salami," he says. "This year we've tried 30 different types." Desserts, however, are his speciality; no matter how full diners are they always find space for one of his creations.

By comparison, Antonella is almost part of a cooking dynasty, one for which she shows appropriate respect. She's continued the long-standing practice of featuring dishes from the restaurant's menu in years gone by and showing the year they first appeared. Former dishes are chosen as they grab the couple, usually prompted by whatever produce is particularly good. However, the *polpetinne* (from 1967) are a permanent feature.

Equally and deservedly popular is the antipasto platter. Whether you're eating in the beautiful, fragrant and colourful garden in the summer, or cosying up to the hearth inside during the winter, you'll soon realise that almost everybody opts to start with this inspired selection of seasonal assortments.

It's no surprise that Dora glows with pride when she discusses her daughter's achievements. But she knows it hasn't been easy. The stress of working in a kitchen is bad enough without the difficulties of entering what, even now, is seen as a male preserve. Antonella laughs about it, but you can see more than a hint of the steely determination and defiance that got her where she is today. "When I first enter other professional kitchens, the men always think of me as the 'signorina'," she says. "It doesn't take me long to show them. I'm small but when I'm in the kitchen, I'm strong. I can lift everything I need to, and all these big men go "Whoa!!"'"

So that's the next chapter. Girl goes to Mauritius, meets boy of her dreams, brings him home, and together they find happiness cooking and serving great food in one of the most acclaimed restaurants in Puglia.

But it's not the last chapter. There's another potential chef in the family. At the age of six, little Shamira is already a *buongustaio*, tucking into both Italian and spicy Mauritian food. She's even got the knack of making *orecchiette*. Proof, perhaps, that she too was born in the kitchen. It surely won't be long before she starts teaching her baby sister Angelica. This story is clearly far from over.

"Sagna penta" di Farina di Ceci con Caponata di Melanzane, Cacio e Menta
Chickpea Pasta with an Aubergine Caponata, Cheese and Mint

Created in 2006, this is a relatively recent addition to the menu, but has proved to be very popular. The chickpea pasta is easy to make and delicious with the vegetables.

SERVES 4

For the pasta:
250g durum wheat flour or semolina
85g puréed chickpeas
10cl extra virgin olive oil
25g chickpea or gram flour
2 eggs, beaten

For the sauce:
15cl extra virgin olive oil
400g aubergine, peeled and the skin julienned and deep fried, and the flesh diced

10g white onion, chopped
1/2 clove garlic, chopped
6 mint leaves and extra leaves for garnish
Salt and pepper
4 cherry tomatoes, deseeded and julienned
20g fresh tomato purée
40g cacioricotta or a matured salty cheese, grated

Mix all the pasta ingredients together. Work the dough well, and roll out into a sheet of about 2mm thick, cut into tagliolini and leave to dry.

Peel the aubergine; julienne the skin and dice the flesh. In a frying pan, heat the oil and gently brown the aubergine cubes. Add the onion, garlic, mint, salt and pepper and mix. When the onions have softened add the tomatoes and the tomato purée and cook for a further two minutes on a high heat. Separately, deep fry the julienned strips of aubergine skin, and keep to one side.

In the meantime, cook the pasta briefly until just al dente, then sauté together with the vegetables for a couple of minutes. Divide between four plates and garnish with the deep fried aubergine skin, the cheese and the mint, and slices of tomato.

Wine suggestion: White — Teresa Manara , Salento IGT, Cantele (Chardonnay)

Bocconcini di Coniglio ai Funghi Misti e Lampascioni Piccanti
Rabbit with Mushrooms and Spicy Onions

Although the original Ricci recipe (from 1998) includes both mushrooms and lampascioni (the bulbs of the hyacinth family which require soaking for many hours before use and are like very bitter onions), the dish works well with either just shallots to replace them or solely mushrooms.

SERVES 4

30cl extra virgin olive oil
400g rabbit fillet, chopped into small pieces
Salt
30cl rosé wine
2 shallots, peeled and quartered
¹/₂ clove garlic, chopped
1 bouquet garni (thyme, bay leaf, rosemary)
100cl vegetable stock
8 cherry tomatoes, skinned
16 *lampascioni* or small peeled shallots or 200g various mushrooms, cleaned and cut
1 fresh chilli, thinly sliced

Heat the oil in a frying pan and brown the rabbit on all sides. Season with salt only. Pour in the wine then mix in the quartered shallots and garlic. Add the bouquet garni and leave to cook for 10 minutes, adding some stock from time to time if needed (some rabbit absorbs a lot and it should not be allowed to dry out).

Add the cherry tomatoes, the *lampascioni* or mushrooms and the fresh chilli, and cook covered until the vegetables are cooked. Remove the bouquet garni and serve steaming hot.

Wine suggestion: Rosé — "Girofle" Salento IGT, Azienda Monaci (Negroamaro)

Cibus Angelo Silibello

via Chianche di Scaranno 7
(Piano Terra di Vecchio
Convento dei Domenicani)
72013 Ceglie Messapica
T: +39 0831 38 89 80
www.ristorantecibus.it

Opening hours: 12.30–14.30;
  20.30–22.30 (May–Sept)
  19.30–22.00 (Oct–Apr)
Closed: Tues
Holidays: last week Jun and first
  week Jul
Covers: 70 restaurant;
  30 conservatory; 30 wine bar

It started with repulsion. Then it became fascination. And now? Now Angelo Silibello and cheese are definitely an item. Not that it happened overnight. Despite a lifetime working with food, it's only in the last 20 odd years that Angelo's ardour has developed. You could say it has matured. In fact today his restaurant boasts one of the best cheese boards in Italy.

Impressive though this may seem, Cibus is about more than just cheese. Puglia is serious about its antipasti of course, but even among profuse competition, Cibus crafts a formidable antipasto platter: *capocollo*, made locally to Angelo's own recipe; a carpaccio of *maialino di latte* with finely cut vegetables; a salad of *grana cappello* (a local grain) with grated *cacioricotta*; and, unsurprisingly for a cheese obsessive, a ricotta soufflé (and perhaps ricotta with toasted almonds).

Is the antipasto Angelo's favourite course? The answer is diplomatic. "All courses are important," he insists. "After an excellent antipasto, you have to follow with a first course and second course of equal standard. But..." Ah yes, the "but". "But my favourite dish is broad bean purée. It's simply marvellous." Spoken like a true Pugliese.

Angelo, also known as Lillino, proudly announces that, since it opened, all the food served has been the restaurant's very own recipes. Nothing wild or wacky, you understand; the dishes are firmly rooted in tradition and built on tried and tested culinary approaches. However, Angelo's philosophy is that the old needs to be respected but traditions need to move on. "*Il nuovo senza il vecchio non si può. Il nuovo deve essere consequenza del vecchio.* The new without the old is impossible". As if to reflect this, the menu changes regularly — and not just for

seasonal reasons. "It's necessary," he says, "necessary for us. To keep us on our toes." Heaven forbid that the Silibello family should become complacent.

Because this is very much a family business. Angelo's parents' opened a restaurant a few hundred metres away in 1952, and his own business, which started 13 years ago, is still a family affair. His mother, Giovanna, now in her mid-70s, continues to cook every day, working in the kitchen with her daughter Filomena. They make a highly efficient team. Giovanna in particular has the air of somebody who has spent a lifetime at the stove: self-assured and never faltering. Admittedly she does have some — how would you describe them? — quirks, perhaps? For instance, when checking hot sauces for seasoning, she places her hand over the pot and then smells it. "It's just my habit. I can tell whether the pan needs more salt or pepper by doing that," she says, smiling serenely.

Cibus of course is two establishments in one, for very good reasons. As Angelo says: "Those who want to come and eat can do that in the restaurant, and people who only want to drink wine and have a light snack can do that" — although 'light snack' hardly does justice to the excellent cheese, ham or salt cod on offer, accompanied by the perfect wine, let alone the wonderful and popular tasting evenings.

Above left: Giovanna, Angelo's mother, continues to cook every day.

Above: Lillino, with one of his prized meat slicers.

Angelo is clearly knowledgeable about wine and what he's done in his wine bar reflects a desire to share that knowledge. With the Slow Food organisation, he has moved from straightforward wine tastings to the more fulsome *laboratorio di gusto* where wines and local specialities are served and enjoyed together. He is also a strong supporter of small producers so you'll find wine at Cibus not easily found elsewhere. You'll even be given the background story to the grape and vineyard.

In fact, all sorts of revelations and insights will be passed on as the plates are served. For instance, did you know that a light, fresh organic cheese comes from the milk of Podolica cows, which are strong and produce very little milk? Such evident fascination with both topics begs the question: which is more important to him, wine or cheese? "They're both equally important," he says, "but I'll also add great beers. There are some wonderful beers made by artisan producers. I've done some interesting *degustazione* with different cheeses, breads and the right wine, beer, or even liqueur. Cheese and grappa is a wonderful pairing." So too, he assures us, is cheese and Guinness.

As for his other passions, one of the small rooms that makes up Cibus is a conservatory, and if you look closely you'll see evidence of the man behind the host: old cameras attest to Angelo's photography hobby, jazz posters reflect his interest in music, and the tambourines offer a big clue as to what he plays. In the Cibus wine bar, there's a large collection of meat slicers, the oldest from 1928, appropriately displayed among the hanging *prosciutti*.

As we approach the final treat on Angelo's acclaimed cheese platter, (moving from the mildest to the strongest as he always advises diners), he talks again about how he would like his children to continue Cibus. "Why not?" he asks. "There are so many doctors and lawyers. There are very few excellent restaurateurs."

He'd love his teenagers to benefit from their parents' — and grandparents' — experience. "Naturally I want them to go to school and university but they may want to carry on with this work," he says. And, after a pause, he adds: "There's a beautiful, sad Sardinian song in which a son tells his father that he knows he's been handed the baggage of experience, but he doesn't know what to do with it. I was lucky. I knew how to use mine."

Melanzane Ripiene di Pasta Pasta-filled Aubergines

As good as this dish is, Giovanna recommends that "it's even better if made and left to rest overnight before serving".

SERVES 2

1 aubergine, washed and halved
  lengthwise
Extra virgin olive oil
1 carrot, peeled and grated
$1/2$ onion, chopped finely
1 clove garlic, chopped finely
4 basil leaves

80g meat (pork is good, as is a mix
  of leftover meats) finely chopped
Salt and pepper
5 ladles runny tomato sauce
120g small pasta shapes, such as
  maccheroncini, sedanani
60g Pecorino, grated

Scoop out the flesh of the aubergine halves and keep to one side. Heat the oil in a deep frying pan and fry the aubergine shells for about 5 minutes. Then turn them over to fry the other side. In the meantime, gently fry the carrot, onion, garlic and half the basil in a separate pan.

When the aubergine shells are cooked, remove from the oil and leave to drain downwards on kitchen paper. Retain the oil on the heat. Cut the removed aubergine flesh in half and fry in the same oil. When soft (after about 10 minutes) and the palest gold, remove it with a slotted spoon and drain.

Add the meat to the carrot mixture and stir in thoroughly over a medium heat. Season to taste before adding a ladle of tomato sauce.

While still warm and before it darkens, blend the cooked aubergine flesh to form a paste. Add this to the carrot and meat mixture on the heat and mix well.

Cook the pasta in salted water. Drain when it is half cooked, bearing in mind that it will finish cooking in the oven. Put in a bowl with the cheese, then ladle in the meat and vegetable mixture and mix thoroughly so that it is evenly combined.

Stuff the aubergine halves with the pasta and meat mixture, place in an ovenproof dish, with a ladle of tomato sauce over each half. Place a basil leaf on top of each half. Put into a preheated oven at 170–180°C for about 15 minutes.

Serve one aubergine half per person with a ladle of warm tomato sauce, garnished with a fresh basil leaf.

Wine suggestion: Rosé — "Girofle" Salento IGT, Azienda Monaci (Negroamaro)

Tasca di Maiale con i Lampascioni
Pork with Onions

This pork dish is served at Cibus with lampascioni, the bulbs, or bitter onions that are a Pugliese speciality and need soaking before use, as they provide a contrast to the sweetness of the pork. Filomena, Angelo's sister who cooks this, recommends the substitution of shallots in their place.

SERVES 4

200g dry breadcrumbs, softened in a small quantity of milk

1kg boned belly of pork, cut lengthwise along the side

100g Pecorino, grated

2 large garlic cloves, crushed

Bunch parsley, chopped

Salt and pepper to taste

2 eggs, beaten

500g shallots, cooked and quartered

Extra virgin olive oil

600g shallots, peeled and roughly chopped

1 garlic clove, crushed

Bay leaves

Salt

White wine, generous splash

Pink peppercorns

Drain the breadcrumbs of excess milk. Mix them in a bowl with the Pecorino, garlic, parsley, salt, pepper, eggs and shallots. Open out the meat and season with salt. Spread the paste along one side and fold the second half over, ensuring that the paste is neatly inside. Sew up the open edge with cooking twine and gently massage so that the stuffing is evenly distributed.

Place in a greased, ovenproof dish, season with salt and pepper and pour over some olive oil. Put in a preheated 180°C oven for 2 hours.

In the meantime, make the onion accompaniment by frying the shallots in the oil with the garlic and bay leaves. Season with salt and leave to cook on a medium heat for about 10 minutes until soft. Mix in the wine so that the shallots become slightly creamy. Remove and discard the bay leaves.

Serve thick slices of the pork, with a spoon of shallots on top. Drizzle extra virgin olive oil over and around the meat and sprinkle with pink peppercorns.

Wine suggestion: Red — "Vigna Lobia" Salento IGT, Botrugno (Negroamaro)

Conversano

Known as the *Città d'Arte*, Conversano offers interesting exhibitions, elegant churches and buildings, an imposing medieval castle and a mo amphitheatre used for concerts in the summer. However, the unoffici daily theatre of the Conversano elders is also worth a look. The old fel settle comfortably outside the relevant organisation, perhaps the *Ass. Naz. Combattenti*, smartly dressed, keeping warm in the sun, passing comment on the world as it goes by and dispensing advice to members of the younger generation as they slow down on their scooters to

Pashà Antonello and Maria Magistà

Piazza Castello 5/7
70014 Conversano
T: +39 080 495 1079
www.pashaconversano.it

Opening hours: 13.00–15.30;
  20.00–24.00
Closed: Tues, and, in winter,
  Sun evening open only by
  reservation
Holidays: no set dates
Covers: 22 inside

Pashà is a title indicating a lordly and, by extension, possibly indolent, figure from Ottoman Empire times. It was also, incongruously, Antonello Magistà's nickname through school. No one is quite sure why. Even as a young man, when he helped out in his father's coffee bar the locals would talk about going to see Pashà. Years later he set up a restaurant on the floor above. What else could he call it?

There was no pressure put on Antonello to follow in his parents' footsteps. The restaurant could almost be called a fluke. After graduating in accountancy and completing his military service, he went to Ferrara to enrol on a law course. Returning home he bumped into his father talking to the architect whose studio occupied the first floor above the caffè. The architect was vacating the premises. "A light bulb went on above my head," he explains. He instantly wanted to develop a restaurant there.

Conversano is a small town — 33,000 inhabitants according to the locals — and by Antonello's account, a fairly reserved one. So reserved in fact that while the locals have been patronising the caffè for over a century, very few have found out what now lies up the stairs — at least not directly. "People who live just around the corner come upstairs for the first time because a work colleague in Bari has recommended us," explains Antonello.

If it's that difficult, why not just open another pizzeria? Simply put, Antonello was convinced that his decision "to open something a bit different to what was already there" would succeed. His belief was based on his own experience. "We want to treat everybody in the way that we would wish to be treated if we went somewhere...to receive all of our guests as warmly as they would be received in a private home. And," he adds, "it has brought good results."

His lack of self-doubt should not be mistaken for arrogance. He is open to suggestions and constantly striving to stay ahead of the game. But that is part of his philosophy. He constantly asks himself: what would I enjoy? What do I look for as a customer?

Having said that, the wall covered in wine bottles may seem a little unconventional at first. However, like the décor generally, it's endearingly quirky and one of the many personal and fun touches that make the mood so relaxed and welcoming.

But what about the food? Who is the chef responsible for the beguiling mix of the modern and traditional that makes Pashà's recipes so special? In fact she was never formally hired. Antonello explains that the restaurant had three chefs in as many years at the start. When the third had to have a knee operation, Antonello asked his mother to step in until he returned. That was six years ago.

Maria Magistà has never had any professional training. And yet, for all that she is self-taught, a lifetime's understanding of flavours, textures and the colours of cooking is manifest in every plate of food she prepares. But, says Antonello, there's more: a ceaseless striving to better understand everything that goes into the preparation of a dish. "I'm always in the kitchen" she says, laughing. "I have no other interests!" Indeed, despite the huge amount of time, sometimes 18 hours a

Antonello strongly believes that "my job is to make customers feel good in every way, not just to provide good food".

day, that she is in the kitchen, she spends every spare moment reading, researching, experimenting — satisfying her curiosity about every aspect of food. She is especially passionate about the region's vegetables. "They're the treasures of Puglia," she says.

Initially, when Maria took over, Antonello thought it prudent to reduce his menu from ten choices per course to three. It was a happy accident. He found it easier to source excellent seasonal produce and to put a huge amount of care into every dish served. Now he's quite scathing about the muddle of tastes served by many places on their large antipasti selections. These days the menu changes every month. But it still offers three choices per course.

People rave about Maria's food. Maria, however, while quietly proud of what she serves, is never complacent. The easy culinary route is not an option. She bakes bread twice a day, before both lunch and dinner, so that it can be served warm. She refuses to buy commercially made *taralli*, making those from scratch too.

As Antonello says: "My mother is uncompromising. For her the morning shop is 70 to 80 per cent of the result. Often she has a list and, whereas I would buy everything at the market, she specifies that the eggs, for example, have to come from another place because otherwise the *crema* won't be good. For every type of

Above left: Maria is uncompromising in her search for top quality produce.

Above: The downstairs caffè where it all began.

raw material there is a reference." She is, he adds, "the soul of this restaurant. No matter how welcome I make people feel, it's the love and passion on the plate that makes people return."

Which is hardly fair on himself — he is, after all, a qualified sommelier. But he prefers to play this down. As he puts it: "It's important that we trust our own tastes, that we don't let ourselves be conditioned by external factors, by external elements — to only like wine that has won lots of prizes. The role of the restaurateur is not to bring an encyclopaedia of wine to the table that the customer will never be able to read before choosing. It is to give to the customer a selection of wines — and also to regularly change things, so that the wine list is dynamic and represents all the regions."

And yet he opens his wines with a theatrical flourish. Ah yes, but that's an integral part of the service, he says. People want to have all their senses satisfied, not just their taste buds. "The look of the plates, the theatre of the wine, the feel of the fabrics...my job is to make customers feel good in every way, not just to provide good food. I like them to be moved emotionally as soon as they enter."

And of course to feel looked after. Antonello doesn't distinguish between Italian and foreign diners at Pashà. He distinguishes between people who live in the area, and those from outside it. He is sensitive to the needs of both groups. The locals won't want a Pugliese dish and local wine if that's what they've been tucking into at home. Visitors from Tuscany, Sicily or abroad, however, want to experience the local food and wine specialities. "We try to provide whatever takes each group's fancy," he says.

The word about Pashà seems to be spreading. But, even as the number of guests grow, the number of covers remains small. "There's the temptation to transfer, to move to another town, to a larger place," says Antonello. "But when I look out of the window, at the sea, the countryside, the castle, I have to ask: where would I go?"

Sitting at one of the front window tables with that memorable view spread out before you, you know where Pashà — the person and the restaurant — belongs. The food, welcome and attitude remain firmly entrenched in the *territorio*; only the name is different.

Minestra di Bietole, Cozze, Pomodorini e Bottarga di Muggine con Crosta di Pane di Altamura

Minestra of Swiss Chard, Mussels, Cherry Tomatoes and Fish Eggs with Toasted Altamura Bread

Maria always makes 10 servings at a time of this. Altamura bread is world renowned, but in its absence, other top quality white breads can be substituted. Maria stores the bread she uses in this recipe for two days in the fridge "so that it becomes soft". She also includes grey mullet roe as she believes they are fish eggs with a particularly delicate taste, but adds: "Other fish roe could be used, or you could omit this ingredient, depending on your individual preference."

SERVES 10

5kg Swiss chard
2kg mussels
10 large slices of top quality bread
2 cloves garlic
Extra virgin olive oil

1kg cherry tomatoes
Grey mullet roe, or tuna roe to taste, optional

Cook the chard in salted water for about 10 minutes on a medium heat until the stalks are soft. Drain, chop and put to one side. Put the mussels in a pan, and heat them as they are, with nothing added, until they are warmed through and open. Discard all that remain closed. Shell the others. Filter the extracted water remaining in the pan and put to one side.

Put each slice of bread around a large metal pastry cutter and put in a preheated 180°/200°C oven for 2–3 minutes so that it becomes a gentle golden colour. Alternatively, prepare toasted fingers.

Put one garlic clove, some oil and the mussels into a pan and warm through gently so that the mussels absorb a slight hint of garlic. In another pan, put some oil, the other garlic clove and the tomatoes. Cook for about 10 minutes on a medium heat, stirring occasionally, before removing the garlic and adding the chard. Mix well. Add the mussels from the other pan and mix everything together. Add the fish eggs now if using. Remove from the heat and serve in a bowl with the bread.

Wine suggestion: White — "Pietra Bianca" Castel del Monte DOC, Tormaresca (Chardonnay, Fiano)

Cartoccio al Forno con Agnello, Patate e Funghi Cardoncelli

Oven Baked Lamb with Potatoes and Cardoncelli Mushrooms in a Parcel

Maria varies this recipe, substituting artichokes, shallots or the bitter lampascioni for the cardoncelli mushrooms.

SERVES 10

200cl extra virgin olive oil	200g Pecorino, grated
Small bunch parsley, chopped	5kg lamb, 3 cuts per person
Garlic (optional and to taste)	(say, chop, shoulder and leg)
10 medium potatoes (1 per person),	10 sheets greaseproof paper
peeled and cut into small pieces	10 strips of tin foil (to secure the
1kg cherry tomatoes, quartered	parcels)
1kg cardoncelli mushrooms,	
cleaned and cut into bite-sized	
pieces	

Preheat the oven to 200°C.

Put the oil, parsley and garlic in a liquidiser and blitz so that, as Maria puts it, you "get the taste without the bits". Coat the potatoes in this mixture and then combine with the tomatoes, mushrooms and Pecorino.

Take 10 deep plates, put a sheet of paper in each one, and put the 3 pieces of lamb into each one, along with a good portion of the vegetable mixture. It's already seasoned so seal the paper with the foil strip, and put all the parcels into the preheated oven for 40 minutes.

Serve one parcel per person, to be opened at the table.

Wine suggestion: Red — "Vandalo" Castel del Monte DOC, Tenuta Cocevola (Nero di Troia)

Foggia

Foggia has been commercially important for centuries and is still the principal communication hub for the north of the region. As a large commercial town it is frequently ignored by foreign visitors to Puglia. This is a pity as its former importance is clearly shown by the number of impressive ancient buildings, including many churches, as well as its museums and archaeological sites.

But it's not just the past that Foggia celebrates. The town boasts an active cultural and artistic community and hosts events such as jazz and independent film festivals.

Chacaito L'Osteria di Zio Aldo
Aldo and Letizia Massimo

via Arpi 62
71100 Foggia
T: +39 0881 708 104

Opening hours: 12.00–15.00;
 20.00–23.00
Closed: Sun
Holidays: 2 weeks in Aug,
 Easter
Covers: 40 inside

Chacaito? "It's the name of an ancient, now extinct Caribbean people, who were so antagonistic that they were named after the aggressive Chaca fish." Not your everyday Italian restaurant name, then.

Aldo Massimo, owner and part-time chef of Chacaito Osteria di Zio Aldo in Foggia, goes on to explain that the original Chacaito was owned by a Venezuelan. "It was the first Venezuelan restaurant in Foggia. He lovingly furnished it in pink with lots of piranha fish decorations, in a Caribbean style." It didn't last.

The name, however, did. Admittedly Aldo put on an impressive show of canvassing opinion by putting 20 likely names on a ballot paper, giving it to his customers and monitoring the results. This went on for about a year after which Ristorante Arpi (the name of the street and the old name of Foggia) was the clear front runner, but in the end he had to admit to himself that he preferred the old name — it was, after all, unique — so he kept it and threw in his own name for good measure.

Aldo was working as a radiographer in those days, so taking over the premises and transforming the interior had to be carried out in his spare time. It sounds tough but he was entitled to 150 days off a year to limit his exposure to radiation. In any case, he typically cooked five times a week at home for friends. So he just moved to via Arpi and started charging them.

And he retired from the world of science. Well, perhaps not entirely. There's a profusion of medical instruments in the kitchen (he says he finds them useful) and, in any case, he loves to study the transformation process involved in cooking. He makes his frittata in the oven with beer, and will offer a commentary on the aspects of the yeast, air and egg proteins that cause the doubling of volume. Or

Aldo loves the scientific aspects of cooking.

he'll explain how his variation on the classic Pugliese *fave* and *cicorie* involves *cicerchie* and grated potato, which acts as a glue. He's even modified his hob so that more gas comes out of it "because the quality of food is 30 per cent dependent on the quality of the fire". In case you were wondering, it all tastes pretty good too. He's as much a chef as a scientist, after all.

Which is why he is fiercely critical of fast food and, aptly, a big fan of *stracotti*. You or I might call it slow cooking. Or possibly very, very slow cooking. He rattles off a list of times as if he's in competition. His *ragù*, you should know, takes eight hours, his *genovese* 12 hours — all on the gentlest of heats of course. They are both worth waiting for, but then waiting is something he's been good at since childhood. Aldo talks nostalgically about crowding around his mother with his siblings "when she fried things in lard. My brothers and sisters and I would take pieces of old bread to catch the hot fat as it fell."

He also remembers how good cooking would transform the most basic ingredients. "For an antipasto, I take bread, soak it, break it into pieces, add cheese, garlic, parsley, salt and pepper, make shapes and fry it. Put it in the tomatoes and eat it. People want to know what it is — I tell them that it's bread! Meatballs without meat!"

In keeping with his medical background, he's also a stickler for cleanliness but, as a traditionalist, he just has to do it his way, the old-fashioned way, with "unrefined soap and elbow grease. I love washing dishes and pans. It gives me huge satisfaction."

Given his strong opinions, you may not be surprised to hear that Aldo will happily talk for hours in an increasingly animated fashion about — well, whatever bothers him. The virtues of storing bread in a pillowcase, his hundred-year-old grandmother's consumption of bread and wine, the battle to retain the Foggia dialect, the modern obsession with cholesterol, the evils of fast food, the joys of King Crimson — he has something to say on all of them.

His daughter Letizia, by contrast, prefers to leave the talking to her father and get on with the job. Letizia started cooking at his osteria 15 years ago when she was 18. She continues doing the lion's share of the defiantly unpretentious work in the kitchen. She's charming and she speaks good English. She may not be the loquacious one, but she likes to throw in the occasional droll observation. She'll wryly tell you that the restaurant is dimly lit and hard to reach by mobile phone signals. Is that a problem? Not, apparently, for the many people who choose it for a romantic dinner and don't want to be interrupted — by their wives for instance...

Above left: The anteroom where Letizia can sometimes be overheard rehearsing.

Above: Letizia calmly gets on with her job.

And she is nothing like as noisy as her father. Well, not always. She and her friends can be very loud, aggressive and threatening. At least they are when using the anteroom to rehearse scenes from Young Frankenstein or Chicago. Like her, they are professional actors.

Aldo's occasional prickliness is far from being an act, of course, but it's the prickliness of a man who loves food, loves his job and just wants to get it right. His customers are happy to play along, sometimes giving him marks out of ten for his efforts — high marks, invariably. But not too high. "If ever anybody gives me a 10, I say that I don't want it," he insists. "Give me eight, give me nine, give me the possibility of doing better!" As far as cooking is concerned, one has never arrived, it seems. "*Nella cucina non si arriva mai, non si finisce mai!*"

Above left: The food at Chacaito is defiantly unpretentious.

Above: The restaurant is dimly lit, but that's part of the appeal for some regulars.

Paccheri con Frutti di Mare e Friarelli
Paccheri with Seafood and Peppers

This is not a typical dish from Foggia, but Aldo is particularly fond of it as "it's a result of my imagination. It's a mixture of several different dishes and I find such concoctions inspiring." Friarelli are small green peppers which are quite sweet and found in Puglia and Calabria.

SERVES 8

Extra virgin olive oil	**500g mixed seafood**
1 clove garlic, chopped	**1 red tomato, very finely chopped**
5 friarelli peppers, chopped	**for final garnish**
Salt and pepper	**Parsley, chopped**
300g paccheri (large pasta tubes)	

In a pan put the oil, garlic and four of the five peppers. Once heated through add the seafood, keep on a gentle heat and mix from time to time. Season.

Separately, boil the pasta. Drain when al dente, add to the seafood pan and mix. Sprinkle over the remaining pepper, the tomato and parsley and serve immediately. If preferred, the seafood can be shelled before serving.

Wine suggestion: Rosé — "Monrose" Puglia IGT, Primis (Montepulciano)

Sfilacci di Mucca Podolica con Verdura
Podolica Beef with Greens

Letizia stresses that this takes no time at all to cook, and indeed it should be done quickly. Aldo uses beef from Podolica cows for this and usually the diaphragm fillet, which he explains "is the tender cut we usually give to the ill and elderly". Sometimes, Letizia substitutes salad leaves for the green vegetables, in which case she simply stirs the raw, washed leaves into a warm pan off the heat.

SERVES 4

Extra virgin olive oil	**500g green leafy vegetables,**
400g beef sirloin, cut into strips	**eg sprouting broccoli, boiled**
Dried chives to taste	**Salt**

Heat the oil in a frying pan and add the meat. Cook over a moderate heat, stirring constantly so that the meat doesn't stick. Add the chives. In another pan, sauté the cooked vegetables in some oil. This should be done quickly just to warm them through and flavour with the oil. Season.

Serve immediately by putting the vegetables on a plate and placing the meat on top.

Wine suggestion: Red — Cacc'e Mmitte di Lucera DOC, Alberto Longo (Nero di Troia, Montepulciano, Bombino Bianco)

Gallipoli

Gallipoli is both a hard-working and picturesque fishing port. The old medieval town is squeezed onto a small island, accessed by an ancient bridge. There is a small retail fish market next to the bridge on the old side. But head to Piazza Aldo Moro and to the left of the lovely Santa Maria del Canneto church to find the altogether more lively wholesale fish market. In the evening, vans noisily toot to announce that fresh fish are arriving. Full polystyrene boxes are carted around — as are lethally endowed swordfish. Try to keep clear of them — and of the hazardous young scooter drivers precariously perching prawns on their footpads.

La Puritate Paolo Fedele

via S. Elia 18
Città Vecchia
73014 Gallipoli
T: +39 0833 264 205

Opening hours: 12.00–15.00;
  20.00–24.00
Closed: Wed (Jun–Sept open
  all week)
Holidays: Oct (all month)
Covers: 35 inside; 45 conservatory

Sunday lunchtime. La Puritate is filled with the beautiful people of Gallipoli, dressed up or (fashionably) dressed down. At the first hint of a sunbeam they all smoothly slip on the most stylish dark glasses.

The restaurant's link with snappy dressing doesn't only come from its clientele, however. Paolo Fedele's grandparents may have run a simple trattoria, but his father, Ernesto, left for a career in fashion.

Retiring from the rag trade, Ernesto was, however, drawn back to his origins. The Fedele family have, after all, been Gallipoli residents for as many generations as anybody can remember. He decided he would open a restaurant. But he had something very specific in mind. He found what he was looking for in Gallipoli's Città Vecchia: a house, with walls dating from the 1600s, overlooking the Ionian Sea. It took a year to convert the private residence into a restaurant. La Puritate opened for business in December 1996.

The restaurant is in the Purità quarter of the old town, next to the Chiesa della Purità and a few steps above the Purità beach. Hence the name, which means purity in Latin and, rather neatly, also applies to what the Fedeles offer: fresh, top quality fish, pure and simple. Ernesto can guarantee this: he's the one who goes to the Gallipoli fish market to buy the day's catch directly from the fishermen. Of course sometimes the fishermen are kept on land by bad weather. No problem: the restaurant has its own boat. You don't stop Ernesto that easily.

And it's Ernesto who will probably greet you when you visit. He'll be sitting at the small desk, from which base he runs the dining room. He is not, however, the restaurant's owner. The restaurant may have been Ernesto Fedele's idea, but he's not keen on the responsibilities of management: La Puritate actually belongs

Clockwise from top:
Ernesto adds the finishing touches
to a couple of dishes.

Paolo, La Puritate's sommelier.

Fish, freshly bought at the
Gallipoli market.

to his son Paolo. Paolo, however, is less easy to spot, possibly because he's dressed identically to the other waiters. Don't be misled by the lack of self-importance, though. As the resident sommelier he is able to deal with all wine enquiries.

Or to recommend the most popular dish, which happens to be the house speciality, *Gamberoni al Sale*. Credit for this goes both to Paolo's father and Daniela, his sister, who works in the kitchen. The cooked gamberoni are served on a large mound of salt grains with lots of extra virgin olive oil and two spoons. Your waiter will show you how it's done: turn the fish round to coat it in the oil and salt, put it on to your plate and eat with your hands. Sandro, the French waiter who speaks English, will happily talk you through the easiest way of gracefully handling this. Alternatively, just look around. You'll probably spot more than one of the regulars tucking in.

It's an unpretentious meal, and that appeals to Paolo, who stresses that the idea behind the restaurant is to keep it simple: he just wants people to eat and drink well. With his father organising the fish buying that leaves Paolo to look after the wine, which is just the way he likes it.

He finished his sommelier course in 2005, but for him that is only part of a continuing love affair with wine. In fact he becomes most animated talking about it. For instance, Paolo doesn't agree with the vogue of drinking red wine with fish. His preferred alcoholic accompaniment to fish is a fizzy white, a *bollicine Franciacorta*, "because it cleanses the palate and then you're ready to try another fish". Sound advice — especially when you consider the size and variety of the house antipasto.

Or you could just take it very slowly. Relax. Perhaps look around. You'll notice that there is a car park and a wall between the restaurant gazebo and the sea. If you're there at dusk when the dimmer switch is turned right down and the candles lit, you'll also see that it attracts a fair number of couples in a romantic mood. Most of the sunglasses will have been put away, but the evening crowd will still be making a fair number of heads turn. Ernesto hasn't totally left behind the fashion world.

Linguine alla Palamita Palamita Linguine

This dish is full of summery flavours. Tuna is a good substitute here, and as this is a primo, a little goes a long way.

SERVES 4

1 clove garlic, skinned and left whole
Extra virgin olive oil
250g palamita or tuna fillets,
  cleaned and cut into strips
4 large ripe red tomatoes, skinned,
  deseeded and julienned

Salt and pepper
250g small linguine
Basil pesto, for decoration
Basil leaves, chopped

In a large, shallow saucepan, heat the garlic in the oil for flavour. Remove the garlic and add the fish. Sauté the fish for a few minutes until golden and crisp, then add the tomatoes and season.

Cook the linguine until al dente. Add to the pan containing the fish and heat everything through together for a couple of minutes. Arrange on plates which have been decorated with the basil pesto and sprinkle over the chopped basil. Serve immediately.

Wine suggestion: White — "Pietra Bianca" Castel del Monte DOC, Tormaresca (Chardonnay, Fiano)

Linguettine alla Puritate
Puritate Linguettine

A simple and delicate dish and one of the most popular primi at La Puritate.

SERVES 6

Extra virgin olive oil

1 clove garlic, peeled and sliced

¹/₂ glass dry white wine

3 small courgettes, washed, trimmed
  and julienned

8–9 cherry tomatoes, quartered

250g small prawns, shelled

3 tablespoons prawn stock

Salt and pepper

Chilli (optional)

250g small linguine

Parsley, chopped

Heat the oil, garlic and wine in a frying pan then add the courgettes and cook gently for a few minutes. Add the tomatoes, shrimps and stock. Season and, if wanted, add some chilli.

Boil the linguine in plenty of salted water and drain when al dente. Add to the pan with the shrimps and briefly heat through.

Serve immediately on individual plates, finishing with a sprinkling of parsley.

Wine suggestion: White — "Messapia" Salento IGT, Leone de Castris (Verdeca)

Lecce

Around every other corner in Lecce is a baroque jewel (*Barocco Leccese*), any one of which on its own would be the main draw of another town — hence the large groups of visitors.

Once you've had enough of sandstone curlicues you might enjoy a trip to the public Garibaldi gardens. However, avoid the hour before dinner when the local schoolkids burn off excess energy on the swings and run amok on roller skates. Alternatively, there are some lovely artisan shops or, for the more adventurous, a lively bar scene that stays buzzing until the early hours thanks to the large student population.

Alle Due Corti
Rosalba De Carlo

Corte dei Giugni 1
73100 Lecce
T: +39 0832 242 223
www.alleduecorti.com

Opening hours: 13.00–14.30;
    20.00–23.30 (reservations
    advised)
Closed: Sun
Holidays: Easter Sunday and
    Monday; 10 days around
    15 Aug; Christmas Day;
    New Year's Day
Covers: 70 inside

Rosalba De Carlo's restaurant is on a site between two courtyards. Hence the name she chose for it: Alle Due Corti. That, however, is the only predictable thing about her.

She was born into high society and became a furrier, an interesting choice of career in one of Italy's hotter regions. Still, when things got difficult she finally had a chance to make a lifelong dream come true: she opened a restaurant. By then, however, she had reached an age when others would be looking forward to a pension. For good measure she ignored haute cuisine and decided that her restaurant would offer recipes barely seen for decades and food that was once the staple of the rural poor. It's a roaring success, of course.

The inspiration for this extraordinary career change came from her childhood, much of which she spent in the kitchen. But, unusually, it wasn't her mother's kitchen that inspired her. It was the mesmerising kitchens of her grandparents' neighbours, the local farming families, where she would watch, wide-eyed, the daily dinner preparations that sowed the seed for Alle Due Corti nearly six decades later.

"Pans were left on the fire all day long so that the chickpeas and other pulses would cook very slowly," she says. "That way they'd completely absorb the surrounding flavours and the scent of the burning wood. Meanwhile, the stew would be cooking in a terracotta pot. When it was mixed together, the result was delicious. They were," she says, "bewitching, happy days."

If she wasn't used to seeing dinner served around five o'clock, she was even less used to seeing whole families seated together round a single large platter on the table, one spoon each, tucking in with enthusiasm. So good was the food that

Above left: Rosalba De Carlo.

Above: One of the seasonal pasta dishes at Alle Due Corti.

even the leftovers were delicious. To this day, Rosalba remembers how Marietta, a mother of 11, "used to make marvellous food by mixing all her leftovers together".

Many years later, these rich, tasty dishes became unfashionable and all but disappeared. In fact in the modern Leccese home, only the elderly are cooking these recipes, partly because only they have the time. Saddened at the decline of so many of these treasured dishes of her childhood, Rosalba decided to do something about it. With her husband Danilo, son Giorgio, a sommelier, and daughter Marinella she is on a mission to bring ancient Salentine cooking to a new audience.

The food is not the only nod to authenticity: the menu is in dialect. This isn't done to be contrary to outsiders, we're assured, but to give atmosphere to the proceedings. However, be grateful that the only other version is in English. And do offer any confused Milanese a hand if they need it; you're probably the best chance they have of knowing what to order without asking.

Of course, being wedded so staunchly to the past means that a near reverence for seasonal changes and availability of local ingredients is part of the job. Rosalba changes her menu pretty much every fortnight. Just as well then that, as Danilo puts it, "she has a library of recipes in her head". And just to make sure, she is also adamant that she should put "the final touch" to every dish served.

Somehow, however, she still finds time to walk around the tables to talk to diners. Offer her a compliment. Go on — she loves it. Yet she genuinely does want to share her stories, answer questions and ensure that if you're after more than just a food experience, you'll get it.

What you'll get, in short, is authentic Leccese dining. But not too authentic. Despite the emotional involvement invested in her restaurant and her desire to be loyal to her source material, her business acumen affirmed that a certain gentrification was required. The hustle and bustle that was a part of Rosalba's inspirational dining experiences has gone, replaced by a relaxed atmosphere; there isn't even background music. The restaurant interior is clean and fresh: straightforward white walls, vaulted ceiling and terracotta flooring. Memorabilia, carefully positioned, adds a pleasing personal touch: quirky, social details, from antiques and personal pictures of Rosalba's grandmother's castle to various heirlooms and bygones from several generations of Danilo's family. There is also a choice of courses and individual servings — and more than just a spoon to dine with.

Their parents may look to the past for inspiration, but Rosalba and Danilo's children are helping to give their memories a modern touch. Giorgio is keen to keep up to date with wine developments, while Marinella has assumed responsi-

The restaurant is found between two courtyards.

Opposite: Rosalba's produce for sale in her restaurant.

Above left: The restaurant interior is straightforward, clean and fresh.

Above: Diners return time and again to enjoy food that was once the staple of the rural poor.

bility for the website and administration. Previously an artist, she now has an active involvement in the business. You will, however, spot one of her glass panels adorning the restaurant. She is helpful, easygoing and, although far less flamboyant than her mother, has the same commitment. It was her idea to promote the sale of some of Rosalba's produce — the sauces, preserves and liqueurs that have been tempting both restaurant and website visitors.

You almost wonder why Rosalba left it so late to start fulfilling her dream. Her answer is surprisingly modest. "If I'd started it earlier, it wouldn't have been a success," she says. "It's only recently that the Salento has been discovered by tourists and that visitors have ventured further south than Bari. Our baroque treasures and coastline are stupendous."

And so, all her visitors agree, is her restaurant. Well, almost all. A local family enjoyed themselves so much there that they returned with their grandmother as a special treat. Big mistake. She was outraged when she saw the menu. "How can you bring me out to eat what I eat every day?" she apparently screamed. There's no pleasing some people.

'Bbinchiamariti

Marinella explains that this dish's name "evokes times gone by: "'bbinchiare" means to satisfy, and "mariti" are husbands. This was a single plate that filled the husband's empty stomach when he returned after a tiring day at work." It's certainly not a light dish and you shouldn't be misled by the use of the term 'frittata'.

SERVES 8

6 large eggs
Salt
200g "00" flour
120g Pecorino cheese, finely grated

Bunch parsley, chopped
Extra virgin olive oil
1 litre runny tomato sauce

Crack the eggs into a bowl, add salt and beat with a fork. Add the flour little by little, mixing continuously to avoid lumps. When the flour is mixed thoroughly, add the cheese and parsley and continue mixing to a batter consistency. Pour the oil into a deep frying pan and when it is hot pour in all the batter and cook like a large frittata. Note that it will tend to swell due to the flour. After about 5 minutes when it has solidified and a crust has formed, turn it over (with the help of a lid) so that the other side can be cooked. When cooked and golden on both sides, remove from the heat and cut into strips approximately 2cm by 7cm.

Pour the tomato sauce into a pan to heat through. When it's nice and hot, gently add the strips of frittata. These should swell further. Leave to cook on a moderate heat for approximately 5–7 minutes. Serve very hot with a sprinkle of Pecorino cheese.

Wine suggestion: Rosé — "Mjère" Alezio DOC, Michele Calò (Negroamaro, Malvasia Nera) or Red — "Varius" Salento IGT, Cantele (Negroamaro, Cabernet Sauvignon, Merlot)

Crostata di Mostarda (Marmellata di Uva)
Jam Tart

Rosalba loves making desserts: "There are so many memories attached to them."
She enjoys making pastry, which is why this recipe is a particular favourite.
It's important that the jam used is not a citrus marmalade; raisin jam is her
preference.

SERVES 10

300g "00" flour
10g baking powder
130g caster sugar
Pinch salt

1 egg, large
120g butter, melted
360g raisin jam, or apple
   or pear jam

Sift the flour into a bowl, then add the baking powder, sugar, salt, beaten eggs and finally the butter. Mix together by hand. Take a shallow, greased cake tin of 25cm diameter and press the dough on the bottom of the dish and up the sides.

Spread the jam evenly on the top of the dough. Roll out long strips of the remaining pastry by hand and lay in a decorative criss-cross pattern across the jam. Put in a preheated180°C oven, for about 20 minutes. When it is golden and resembles a biscuit, it is done. Serve cold.

Wine suggestion: White Dessert — "Paule Calle" Salento IGT Passito, Candido (Chardonnay, Malvasia Bianca)

Cucina Casereccia "Le Zie"
Anna Carmela Perrone

via Col. Costadura 19
73100 Lecce
T: +39 0832 245 178

Opening hours: 12.30–14.30;
  20.00–23.00 reservations
  advised.
Closed: Sun evening and Mon
Holidays: last week Aug and first
  week Sept; 1 week at Easter;
  Christmas
Covers: 45 (inside)

"If you were to eat in a Leccese home, this is traditionally what you'd be given." Anna Perrone offers a handy image for Trattoria Cucina Casereccia. It's certainly a homely restaurant. The interior is basic. The furniture is past its best. It is situated in one of the less lovely streets a few steps outside the centre of Lecce. The food on offer is indeed the type of thing that a lot of locals might eat at home.

And yet it's packed. And not just packed, but packed with locals. And not just locals but noisy locals, some in small gatherings of friends, some in large groups, all crammed in together in a lively, buzzing tableau.

So, why is this restaurant so popular — especially in a town like Lecce, which is home to plenty of busy professionals? That, however, is the answer. They're too busy to cook. When you love home cooking but have no time to prepare your own food, what do you do? You go somewhere that gives you home cooking — in every sense. Not only does Anna serve and fuss over you as if you were at home, but the food on offer is traditional Salentine fare: ingredients like dried tomatoes, aubergines, pepper, rocket and mint ("used a lot in Salentine cooking," says Anna) and standards like pasta with chickpeas (*ciceri e tria*), broad beans with chicory (*fave e cicoria*) and Anna's famous preserved tomatoes.

The fear of losing these culinary traditions has, explains Anna, led to people like her being encouraged to hang on to them. "The Pugliesi don't want to lose their culinary traditions; we'll do all we can to hold on tightly," she says. And she's certainly doing what she can. The menu changes seasonally of course, but nothing extra is added to the traditional recipes and everything — even the wine — is sourced in the Salento.

In August local farmers prepare boxes of tomatoes for her, and then all

hands are on deck to make the necessary supply of *conserva*. Her mother makes the dried tomatoes for winter consumption by putting them in the sun with salt "because that's something of a speciality here". The extra virgin olive oil comes from her mother too and, says Anna, when that runs out, she goes to her cousin. Keeping it in the family? No, keeping it in the *territorio*. "The taste of oil changes depending on the zone of production, and one's palate becomes accustomed to a particular oil," she explains. Luckily her cousin has the plot next door to Anna's mother.

That is not the limit of Anna's mother's influence, however. "When we were very young, and Mamma made her recipes," she says, "we'd all be around the table helping her. It was a game for us, but it meant that I learnt how to do everything. It was an authentic school. I've never been to chef's school; it was a life school."

Anna is far from precious about what she produces, but "only women touch my food, and I prefer it that way". By this she means that no men work in her kitchen — and especially no Salentine men. "Men of the Salento only want to do roasts and barbecues," she says. "It's not easy to teach them other, more subtle ways of cooking."

Men clearly do have some uses, however. Pino, her husband, helps to serve and looks after the accounts "and those critical but boring things that just don't interest me".

Anna offers traditional Salentine home cooking.

Cucina Casereccia is laid-back and informal but does have a reverence for traditional Salentine food. Is that a problem for non-Italians? Apparently not. Outsiders, especially foreigners, are not only given a warm welcome but the opportunity to encounter Leccese food in context. Given that Anna not only heads up the kitchen but the dining room, over the years she's become more than used to dealing with tourists.

"Sometimes it's embarrassing because I don't speak any foreign languages," she says, "but I'll ask: "*Degustazione di cucina salentina*?" and they're always ready to accept that. Foreign guests often don't understand or know our cooking so we ask if they'd like a small taste of all the dishes. They don't have the awkwardness of having to choose, and it's fun to try a little of everything."

But after you've found exactly the right dishes, how do you round off your meal? Coffee is never an option; there's no coffee machine. There is, however, a novel, and delicious alternative. Homemade liqueurs flavoured with lemon and bay leaves are proudly suggested as an aid to digestion. After which, if you still crave an espresso, a wander through Lecce is always pleasant and a source of coffee never far away.

Anna has clearly hit upon a winning formula, and she won't tamper with it.

Anna heads up both the kitchen and dining room.

Opposite: Simply prepared, locally grown produce.

The restaurant is now more than 40 years old but, when Anna took it over eight years ago, she changed very little of it physically. She did, however, add a wardrobe at the entrance so that guests have somewhere to put their coats, and her personal pictures now hang on the walls. A poster of artichokes, olives, wine and oil "reminded me of my homeland when my husband, who's Roman, and I lived in Rome when we were first married". There are numerous photos of old Lecce before the Roman amphitheatre was excavated and cards from visitors. There's also a shot of Anna and Francis Ford Coppola who dropped in for dinner with some friends one night when we were there — and not for the first time, apparently. "He's American but really Italian," says Anna affectionately, delightedly pointing to the shot of her and the great man on the wall.

One more thing. Don't call it the Trattoria Cucina Casereccia. It's better known as Le Zie. What does Le Zie mean? Let Anna explain. "I take care of everybody. And that makes people relax. They don't feel as if they're in a restaurant, they feel as if they're at somebody's home. I want to make sure they're eating, that they're happy, and that's the sort of care and affection that an aunt would show." Le Zie means The Aunties. A Leccese home from home.

Above left: Anna Perrone, who is being encourged to hold on tightly to her culinary traditions.

Above: Cucina Casereccia gives the opportunity to encounter Leccese food in context.

Opposite: A homely restaurant which is regularly packed out with diners who love Anna's home cooking.

Taieddha

This is a classic Pugliese recipe and the name refers to the dish in which it is baked. There are several different spellings, and various ingredients can be used to form the layers. Anna's favourite is with mussels and although she removes the half shell from them still raw, it's both easier and safer for the domestic cook to heat them through first.

SERVES 6

2kg mussels, cleaned

1.5kg potatoes, peeled and cut into medium slices

500g courgettes, cut into medium slices

5–6 medium red tomatoes, cut into small pieces

2 large cloves garlic, finely chopped

Bunch parsley, finely chopped

3 onions

Salt and pepper to taste

50g Pecorino, grated

150cl extra virgin olive oil

110g breadcrumbs

Put the mussels with a small amount of water on the heat so that they cook enough to open. Keep the cooking liquid to one side. Discard any mussels that remain closed. Remove the top shell so that all the mussels are left in the half shell and put to one side. In a large bowl mix the potatoes, courgettes, tomatoes, garlic and parsley together by hand. Coarsely grate one onion into the mixture. Season. Add the cooking liquid from the mussels.

Take a large greased baking dish and roughly slice the remaining, peeled onions into it. Put half the mixed vegetables on top. Take the mussels in the half shell and arrange on top of the vegetables, shell facing downwards. Sprinkle half the cheese over the top and cover with the remaining vegetables. Add a couple of glasses of water (the potatoes need this to cook). Sprinkle over the rest of the cheese. Drizzle over the olive oil, then cover with the breadcrumbs. Put in a pre-heated 200°C oven for 50–55 minutes. Check from time to time and cover with foil if necessary. Test that the potatoes are cooked. Serve hot from the oven.

Wine suggestion: Rosé — Five Roses Salento IGT, Leone de Castris (Negroamaro, Malvasia Nera)

Pasta e Ceci

Pasta and Chickpeas

"Ciceri e tria" is the more usual name for this ancient Leccese dish, but Anna likes to keep it simple. This is her favourite dish "because I adore pasta and pulses".

SERVES 6

500g dried chickpeas, soaked overnight
Salt
2 cloves garlic
1 stick celery
2 bay leaves
500g "00" flour
Water as required
200cl extra virgin olive oil
Freshly ground black pepper

Cook the chickpeas in salted water (the salt helps the skin to stay attached) with the garlic, celery and bay leaves (which aid digestion of the chickpeas) for about an hour or until done. Periodically remove the scum while cooking.

In the meantime, make the pasta using the flour and water but no eggs. Roll out the pasta, leave to dry for 30 minutes and then cut into small, short rectangular strips. Fry ¼ of the pasta in the oil and boil the rest briefly so that it is slightly undercooked.

Sauté the fried pasta, the boiled pasta and the chickpeas very quickly in a frying pan. Serve immediately with freshly ground black pepper.

Wine suggestion: Rosé — Five Roses Salento IGT, Leone de Castris (Negroamaro, Malvasia Nera)

Martina Franca

An enchanting little town in the Valle d'Itria, Martina Franca is blessed with a truly delightful piazza and features (rightly) on many tourist itineraries. However, the Martinese, as the locals are called, retain their grip on the town's character and never let the visitors take over. The numerous baroque and rococo buildings provide a magical backdrop to daily life, including the enthusiastic *passeggiata*. As friendly and welcoming as the Martinese are, you'll find little quarter given if you try to go against the flow along the narrow and winding Corso Vittorio Emanuele.

Ciacco Cristina Lauria

via Conte Ugolino 14
74015 Martina Franca
T: + 39 080 480 0472
www.ristoranteciacco.it

Opening hours: 12.30–14.30
(only with reservation);
 19.30–23.30
Closed: Sun evening and Mon;
 open all week during Aug
Holidays: no set dates
Covers: 40 inside, on two floors;
 16 outside on the roof terrace
 (Jun–Aug, evenings only)

Just inside the entrance to Ciacco, there's an old cookery book on display. Dating from 1934 it belonged to the grandmother of the restaurant's owner, Cristina Lauria, at a time when such books had a role that went well beyond mere reference. Cristina, who is Martina Franca born and bred, explains that there is an old Martinese saying: "If you don't know how to make *orecchiette*, you'll never get a husband."

Times may have changed but even now the book is not just there for decoration: the kitchen still uses it for traditional recipes such as shortcrust pastry, quince jelly and jams. And as a reminder of how things were once done. "Today restaurants can easily buy partly prepared products," Cristina says, "but we do everything from scratch: the *tarallini*, the pasta, desserts, pastries. We do everything from flour, butter and the basics. We don't use anything that's been started elsewhere or convenient."

And they use very little that isn't Martinese. Even Cristina's cooks are Martinese. As for the food...well, Cristina is a strong advocate of local produce. Take the antipasto. One constant component of the antipasto platter is the Martinese meat speciality, *capocollo*. It comes from two acclaimed producers in town.

Cristina is also keen on local culinary traditions. However, tradition gets the occasional tweak. For example, there's an onion focaccia, also part of the antipasti selection, which is typical of Martina Franca except that Ciacco's version is lighter: the onions are stewed rather than fried in fat. And how is this attack on

tradition received? "We try to serve it all year, because if we don't we get told off."

And the *taralli* served at Ciacco are darker than usual. This is because they are made with red wine, not the customary white. It's more time-consuming to prepare but it's definitely worth the wait.

Then there's the *tortelloni* of *grano saraceno* (buckwheat) filled with local greens, sautéed with anchovies and breadcrumbs. Or a purée of broad beans presented differently, say with a crêpe filled with chicory. Or something adapted from one of the many cooking courses Cristina still attends. "Last week I did one on desserts and cakes," she says. "They used lots of foreign products: Asian spices and tropical fruits. But there was one recipe I've adapted to work with our produce: I've turned it into a crunchy *millefoglie* of Altamura bread with sweet ricotta, dried figs, candied orange, and a vincotto sauce. It's delicious."

It's already popular too, like her restaurant. But it's not just the food that inspires such loyalty. Cristina works hard on the whole package: the food, the welcome and the atmosphere. In fact that's pretty much what brought her into the restaurant business. She had waited on tables for a time, but it wasn't until she became disillusioned with her chosen career, law, that she found her true calling. She was at something of a loose end. Her husband needed help running a restaurant and "I found myself doing a job that I liked".

"There's a true pleasure in serving these *orecchiette* in a familiar, welcoming setting," she says. "It's like entering a home. You find everything that you'll find in a home: the warmth and the tenderness. It's not just about the eating."

She is especially happy that when people leave they "don't just say that they had good food, but that they had a good time". And they do, not least because chatting to people is what Cristina excels at. She constantly participates in the menu choices, studying and tweaking the dishes or coming up with new challenges for her talented staff, but her real strength lies in interacting with customers. "I never just put a menu on the table," she says. "I always go to explain to people, to answer their questions and to engage with them."

Why a restaurant in this building? It is by no means one of the bigger establishments in the area, after all. "I had a pizzeria before, and I wanted somewhere more welcoming where I could do something of better quality", says Cristina. "Then I found this place. It was a house where a very old lady used to live."

In fact she found it half converted. A wealthy businessman had bought the house to turn it into a restaurant, but he lost interest. Cristina, however, didn't, even though it meant sorting out the flooring, the kitchen, the bathrooms and the furniture, not to mention all the permits, licences and other paperwork.

Structurally, though, it's still the home it once was. There are one or two other indications of its previous life as well, like the former owner's painting of

the Madonna on the first floor. Then there's the access to the roof. Even though it is now employed during the summer months as a terrace with a fine view of the rooftops and chimneys of the old town, you still have to work your way up three flights of stairs to reach it.

The rest of the time, the inside is a huge draw. In fact Cristina believes that the restaurant comes into its own in the winter. The fireplace, especially in the colder weather, is the cosiest, most sought-after spot, although to many foreigners it's a delightfully cool respite from the heat in high summer.

In fact the only thing that isn't homely and welcoming is the restaurant's name. Cristina chatted to friends and acquaintances about good names for her new venture. Her paediatrician suggested the name Ciacco, and it instantly appealed. Ciacco turns up in Dante's Divine Comedy as a glutton, or as Cristina puts it, "he invited himself to all sorts of meals, tucking in without paying!"

Still, no one takes it personally. How could they? They don't just come here to eat. Cristina was once asked to arrange a private party for a doctor's 50th. "His wife couldn't invite 20 people to celebrate at her house so she invited them here. She told me that she liked the idea of going to a restaurant that felt like her home. That's why people keep coming back."

Above left: The entrance to Ciacco which was formerly a private house.

Above : Cristina's dessert of ricotta, biscuits and chocolate chips.

Overleaf: Cristina Lauria.

Composta di Purè di Fave
Broad Bean Purée

*'Ncapriata, or Fave e Cicoria, is one of the classic Pugliese dishes: dried, cooked
and puréed broad beans served with cooked chicory and abundant olive oil. This
is Cristina's variation, which serves the bean purée with other good vegetables in
season; fried green peppers or onion rings are particular favourites of hers.*

SERVES 6

250g dried broad beans

**2 medium potatoes, peeled and
sliced**

1 teaspoon salt

100ml extra virgin olive oil

To serve: assorted vegetables

Soak the broad beans for an hour before cooking. Put the beans in a pan and
layer the potato slices on top. Add water to a finger's width above the potatoes.
Bring to the boil and leave to simmer gently for about 30 minutes and then drain
off whatever little cooking water is left. Cover the vegetables with fresh water,
add salt and leave on a low heat for about an hour so that the water is absorbed.

The mixture should have become very soft. Gradually mix in the oil with
a wooden spoon to result in a smooth paste. This should be done by hand.

Serve the purée with boiled greens and other vegetables of your choice.

Wine suggestion: Rosé — "Negroamaro" Salento IGT, Cantele (Negroamaro)

Bocconotto

Bocconotto is a typical Martinese (from Martina Franca) dessert, of sweet pastry filled with pastry cream and bitter cherries. It is very sweet and rich so only a small portion is needed.

SERVES 8

For the pastry:
450g "00" flour
150g caster sugar
180g butter
2 whole eggs
1 egg yolk
Vanilla essence, a few drops to taste

For the pastry cream:
4 egg yolks
3 tablespoons caster sugar
2 level tablespoons flour
Vanilla essence, a few drops
½ litre full fat milk

100g bitter cherries in syrup
  or a few spoons of cherry jam
+ 1 egg for glaze
Icing sugar
Cinnamon sticks for garnish

Make the pastry and leave to rest in the fridge wrapped in greaseproof paper for 1 hour.

To make the pastry cream: in a saucepan, off the heat, mix the egg yolks and caster sugar with an electric whisk. Add the sifted flour and vanilla essence, continuing to mix. Slowly add the boiled milk, mixing continually, taking care not to form any lumps. Put the saucepan on a gentle heat and mix until the cream has become quite thick; if it's too runny, it won't hold in the tart.

Leave to cool.

Roll out the pastry to about 1/2cm and line a greased and floured deep tart dish of approximately 25 cm in diameter. Trim the edges. Place the cooled cream in the tart case, and put the cherries on top.

Cover with another sheet of pastry, carefully sealing the edges. Brush with beaten egg. Put in a preheated 180°C oven for 40 minutes. Bocconotto should be served lukewarm and sprinkled with icing sugar.

Wine suggestion: Dessert — Moscato di Trani DOC, Nugnes (Moscato Reale)

Il Ritrovo degli Amici Anna Ancona

corso Messapia 8
74015 Martina Franca
T: +39 080 483 9249

Opening hours: 12.30–15.00;
  19.30–24.00
Closed: Sun evening and Mon
  (Sept–Jun); always open end
  Jun–end Aug
Holidays: mid Jan–mid Feb
Covers: 28 inside; 18 outside

Walking up the delightful plant-strewn path that leads to the door of Il Ritrovo degli Amici, you feel as though you're entering a private residence. Cross the threshold and the feeling gets stronger. It's a small, civilised and serene place. Don't be fooled though. It is the home not only of a mischievous party animal, but of a sentimental, affectionate, emotional whirlwind, a free spirit and a chef praised by her peers within and beyond the region.

And all four of these are one person: the restaurant's owner Anna Ancona. Except that, to her, it's not a restaurant. The name gives it away: Il Ritrovo degli Amici — the place where friends find each other. "The name was no accident," she says. "That's the way it's turned out. Often people will come here for Sunday lunch, they'll be finishing up mid-afternoon, and they'll speak to friends who'll say they're on their way to join them because they've already eaten but they love my desserts. So here I am at 7pm, still serving the Sunday lunch crowd."

Anna bought number 8 Corso Messapia in 1993. "I fell in love with the railings and the little path. I didn't know anything about the inside." People told Anna she was mad to think about setting up a restaurant in such a small space. She bought it anyway.

And it certainly is small: eight tables inside and a few more in a courtyard that offers a secluded spot for outside eating in the summer. And yes, she has to turn away diners, but it's not an issue. "I've always said that I didn't want more than ten tables. I do occasionally fantasise about how wonderful it would be to have just the one."

That's because she likes to pamper each table. She has instant recall of all her regulars' quirks, foibles and preferences. She knows for instance who wants a bowl

of pasta served almost as soon as they sit down. She knows that Cristina is allergic to pepper. She can even remind Pietro, who has just ordered the local speciality of *bocconotto* for a birthday celebration, that he doesn't like cherries.

And she'll immediately organise a delicious alternative, even though she doesn't have a huge amount of help in her kitchen. But then she doesn't think much of modern catering courses. "If you come to my kitchen straight from college, you'll only know how to work in one sector — either *primi* or *secondi*," she complains. "When I'm in the kitchen I move, and I want to know why others can't get their feet going. If you begin by cooking in a house with lots of people, that's how you work."

Which is exactly what Anna did. "Our house was very big, so a gathering of 30 wasn't out of the ordinary. When my husband and I first invited people over for Christmas, we started with 25 and one year 56 of us ate together."

Hence her treatment of customers as if they were friends visiting her home — although few friends would take the sort of liberties some of her regulars get away with. For instance, they often phone to reserve not only a table, but a specific dish "and if I say that's not on the menu, they persist until I agree to make it. It's hard to say no."

Anna, who can't understand why some kitchen staff find it difficult to get their feet going.

Nevertheless, she likes to amaze her clients, and, as that's difficult if they've ordered before they arrive, the obvious target is the interior. In fact last year's holiday was spent redecorating. This attention to detail extends to the garden (she loves tending to the plants in her courtyard and entrance) and even art. A painting of three old men hangs in the restaurant with her signature on it: Vittorianna.

The visual is clearly important to her — before Il Ritrovo degli Amici she worked in graphic design and the fashion industry — up to and including the presentation of her food. Sometimes she may prefer plain white crockery "because I want the contents of the plate to jump out visually". At other times, she'll insist that everything is coordinated: the plates, the candles, the flowers. And she loves flowers. "I bought 250 roses for a birthday party. I wasn't asked to but I thought they'd look good." She also gets really carried away by candles: "If you come here at Christmas, you'd weep: we only illuminate the place with candles at Christmas, about 250 of them. It's very atmospheric."

Her recipes get the occasional makeover too, although she keeps things simple and true to the integrity of the base ingredients. So, for instance, when the mushrooms arrive, Anna will play around with them and some pasta, and offer her new dish to her regulars. If the plates come back spotless, then on to the menu — a verbally delivered rather than printed one — it goes.

Few things make Anna happier than spotless plates being returned to her kitchen. And that's no mean feat; her portions are generous. Not that she plans to change this, of course. "People don't come here to nibble," she says. "They come here because they're hungry. They expect a certain portion size. I could never let myself offer nouvelle cuisine."

What she does offer is made from ingredients supplied locally, from Martina Franca, and as she's a Martina native, you just know that if something is in short supply, she'll charm her way to the top of the queue. "I can get most things from just outside the city walls," she says. "There are some farmers who love me and harvest whatever I need."

She also offers a rather good selection of wine and spirits. In fact she's been invited to join Women in Wine so her recommendations are usually worth following. As for spirits... "We could seat another four people at the table where all the bottles of grappa sit," she says, "but I don't like that idea. People tell me they like that table."

It may seem a bit odd to reduce an already small dining area simply because the customers enjoy looking at bottles of hard liquor. That, however, for Anna Ancona is the point.

She will go to endless trouble for other people. Her son, father of her two adored grandchildren (when the first arrived, she wept for hours with the emotion

Clockwise from top left: Anna's design and artistic background means that the presentation of food is important to her.

Wines, and spirits, are on display in various places around Il Ritrovo degli Amici.

The restaurant is small, but that's the way Anna likes it.

of it), is at the other end of the country in Milan. When he was 40, she flew there and surprised him at his front door, took him out to lunch and then flew home.

And that's the reason her customers come from all over the region, from Vieste, Taranto, Lecce and Trani: to eat her food, of course, but mainly to experience her hospitality. All of this explains why she states matter of factly: "I have nothing in my pocket, but I'm the richest woman in the world. My reward is seeing how happy people are. It gives me the energy to do more. When I see people get up from the table — and I can feel it, my skin feels it — when they leave and they hug me goodbye and it's clear in their eyes that they've had a good time, that inspires me."

"People like it here and they feel comfortable because I give them passion and love," says Anna. "I honestly don't think that there's anything else to it." Small, civilised and serene? The restaurant yes; the owner fails on the last point, and thank heavens for that — long may she dance to her own tune.

Above left: Anna Ancona at Il Ritrovo degli Amici.

Above: A delicious chocolate cake with an orange cream.

Opposite: Anna has a fondness for candles and roses.

Tortino di Melanzane
Aubergine Tortino

Egg-based dishes are a particular favourite of Anna's. There's often one on her menu, featuring good seasonal vegetables that take her fancy. She regularly has fun with garnishes when plating these up and would encourage you to do likewise.

SERVES 4

1 aubergine, finely diced	50g Parmesan, grated
Extra virgin olive oil	2 large eggs, beaten
1 clove garlic, peeled	Small bunch basil, chopped
5 cherry tomatoes, cut into pieces	

Heat the oil in a pan, brown the garlic, then remove and add the aubergine. Once the aubergine has softened, add the tomatoes and stir. Leave on a gentle heat for about 10 minutes, until everything is soft and well cooked. Remove from the heat and leave to cool slightly for about 15 minutes.

Add the Parmesan, eggs and basil. Mix well. In the meantime, grease and flour four aluminium moulds of about 7cm diameter, and fill halfway up. Put in a bain-marie in a preheated 180°C oven for 15 minutes or until set.

Remove from the moulds and serve hot or cold with your choice of garnish.

Wine suggestion: White — "I Sierri" Salento IGT, Cosimo Taurino (Chardonnay, Malvasia Bianca)

Costine al Forno con Patatine Novelle
Oven Baked Lamb with New Potatoes

Anna sources great lamb from nearby and believes that it's so good it should be enhanced by a few herbs, not masked by competing flavours.

SERVES 4

8 lamb chops	**900g new potatoes**
Salt and pepper	**1 tbs dried rosemary**
Dried oregano to taste	**1 tbs thyme, chopped**
Extra virgin olive oil	

Flavour the chops by mixing the salt, pepper and oregano with the oil and rubbing into the meat. Leave to rest at room temperature for 30 minutes. In the meantime, boil the potatoes in lightly salted water for 20 minutes, drain, sprinkle with rosemary and thyme and leave to one side.

Put some oil in a pan and once heated add the chops and brown on both sides. Add the herbed potatoes and a stream of oil and put in a pre-heated 200°C oven for a maximum of 15 minutes. When the potatoes are nicely browned serve immediately.

Wine suggestion: Red — Primitivo di Manduria DOC, Attanasio (Primitivo)

Monopoli

Monopoli has something for everyone. There's the large Piazza Vittorio Emanuele II, whose trees provide shade for the social gatherings of the men of the town who congregate with their own chairs. Take a pleasant walk from there down Largo Plebiscito (with surprises at every turn as old buildings appear), and you'll enter the much smaller Piazza Garibaldi with its relaxing, sheltered caffès, adjacent to the working port. Less relaxed but worth visiting is the lively market, where fishmongers vocally compete with greengrocers. The town also boasts some small but attractive (and clean) beaches.

Lido Bianco Giovanni and Florinda Bini

via Procaccia 3
70043 Monopoli
T: +39 080 887 6737

Opening hours: 12.00–15.30;
  19.00–23.30
Closed: Mon (except Aug)
Holidays: Jan (all month)
Covers: 250 inside; 50 outside

"A dining terrace by the sea should be like this. It shouldn't be elegant. It should be clean and beautiful. It should feel part of the sea."

Giovanni Bini isn't exaggerating. Monopoli's Lido Bianco really is a restaurant in harmony with its location. And what a location it is. Sitting in the glass-wrapped dining room just above the Porto Bianco beach with the windows open, you can look down on the Adriatic, hear the sound of the waves crashing against the rocks and see the bathers frolicking below.

In fact from the moment you walk through the front door and see the glorious fish counter, it's hard not to be swept up by the experience. The gleaming display of highlights from that morning's or evening's catch, a long-standing feature of the establishment, is a big draw — even for the locals.

Compared to the magnificent setting, the menu may seem a touch prosaic. That, however, is its appeal. With fish this good, simple cooking is not the easy way — it's the only way. And it's certainly popular; ask any of the large number of regulars pausing at the counter on their way to be seated.

This is good, unfussy food with fresh fish at its centre, thanks largely to Giovanni, who was a sailor before deciding in 1979 to take over the restaurant that his father had run. But he is matter-of-fact about his contribution. "I know my fish. I'm good at selecting top quality produce but I've never learnt to cook," he says. "And I'm not unhappy about that," he adds, although at busy times you may spot him pausing at the big fireplace to turn over fish on the grill rack.

The fish is served with vegetables or the freshest of salads, all cultivated nearby and bought from the market in Fasano, where Giovanni lives, as does the calm, friendly and helpful person who handles the general administration, is the

first point of contact, takes reservations and plans menus for all manner of parties held in the restaurant. She jokes that Giovanni can be a bit stuck in his ways but, as they've been married for a long time and have brought up three sons together, Florinda doesn't really mind. And Giovanni has nothing but praise for his wife who somehow juggles working in the restaurant, organising the family and participating in considerable voluntary work — for the Red Cross and AIDS charities among others.

Florinda affectionately teases that her husband is a traditionalist "who never, ever wants to change anything". In fairness, it only took him a few years to completely transform what is now the main dining room. Just as well, really. Twenty years ago, it was completely open, or as Giovanni says wryly: "When it rained, we had problems."

That development was clearly one both partners were happy with. The couple have, however, for many years disagreed about the flooring. It's currently made up of bold red and white square tiles. Florinda says it hurts her eyes: she is determined that one day it will be pure white wood. You rather think she'll get her way. After all, her tenacity has succeeded in getting Giovanni to listen to some of the research done by their consultant Graziano. Then, again, he is their son.

The glorious fish counter at Lido Bianco, with its gleaming display of the day's catch, is a big draw.

Graziano, however, takes nothing for granted. His job as he sees it, is to be the eyes and ears of the customers, not just through his work in Lido Bianco but by monitoring developments and trends in the restaurant world.

One change they've all noticed in recent years is the tendency for people to opt for red wine with their fish. Like many other Pugliese restaurateurs, Giovanni isn't entirely sure he approves, but he offers a good — and ever-increasing — choice of reds. Keeping his customers happy is a major concern for him. It even extends to offering a modest selection for diners perverse enough to prefer meat to the tempting cornucopia of piscatorial highlights on show. Is there anything Giovanni won't do for his customers? "I don't like football," is the surprising answer, so forget about discussing the match...

Instead, why not pop outside? Florinda designed the delightful outside terrace, a few plant-adorned steps up from the main dining area. On a bright, sunny day, the wooden decking, the white fabric chairs, the deep blue sea dotted with bobbing white yachts in the distance and the shoals of small fish swimming past in the clear water form a glorious scene. Simple, but enough to inspire a feeling of wellbeing in even the most jaded viewer.

The sun isn't always so friendly, though; even with the protection of one of

Above left: Charming service on a sunny day.

Above: The delightful outside terrace was designed by Florinda.

Opposite: The big fireplace has a large grill, perfect for simple cooking.

the many parasols dotted around the terrace it's far too hot to eat there during the high summer days. But get hold of a table on the terrace at twilight and you'll instantly fall under the spell cast by the candles and gentle breeze. There's always the chance that celebrations will be going on somewhere near and that you'll get the added magic of a firework display reflected in the water.

You just find yourself saying it over and over again: what a location. Florinda puts it best. "People don't just come here for the food but for the sea as well," she says. "It really is the combination of both. Diners love being this near to the sea and watching the waves. It's the perfect background music. Even when it's rough, it's a captivating sight."

Below left: Evening dining on the outside terrace is popular with the locals.

Below: Giovanni Bini.

Tubettini alle Cozze con Pomodoro Fresco
Pasta with Mussels and Fresh Tomatoes

This is one of the most popular dishes at Lido Bianco and is also Florinda's favourite "because it's very simple and respects our culinary antiquity. All the flavours and smells of this are ours." In keeping with tradition there is also a refusal to give any quantities, just the strong belief that you should use what you have and in the proportions that make you happy. For instance, some people prefer this with a lot of liquid, almost like a soup, and others prefer it much drier. Adjust to your own taste.

Mussels, cleaned
Garlic, finely chopped
Extra virgin olive oil
Fresh tomatoes, deseeded and
  roughly chopped

White wine
Salt and pepper
Tubettini (or another small,
  short pasta)
Parsley, finely chopped

Put the mussels in a pan with some water and heat until they open. Discard any that remain closed. Leave to cook slightly and shell. Fry the garlic in the oil, add the tomatoes and cook for a few minutes until softened. Add the mussels, white wine and season. Put to one side. Cook the pasta in abundant salted water, remove from heat when barely al dente, drain and add to the pan with the mussels. Shake up so that everything mixes, add the parsley and serve in a bowl.

This can be served with *olio santo* (extra virgin olive oil suffused with chillies).

Wine suggestion: White — Locorotondo DOC, Cantina del Locorotondo (Verdeca, Bianca d'Alessano, Fiano) or Red — "Elo Veni" Salento IGT, Leone de Castris (Negroamaro)

Grigliata Mista di Pesce
Mixed Grilled Fish

It doesn't really matter what fish are used for this, but it is important to use a variety, based of course on whatever is best out of what is available. The chefs at Lido Bianco sometimes use their own pinzimonio instead of olive oil.

SERVES 1

Four different fish, such as
  1 squid
  1 cuttlefish
  1 large prawn
  1 bream or sea bass

Extra virgin olive oil
White wine vinegar, handful of
  chopped parsley or celery leaves,
  salt and pepper (optional)

Preheat the grill to very hot. Either brush the fish with olive oil or a variation on *pinzimonio* (mix the oil, vinegar, parsley or celery leaves, salt and pepper). Put on the grill and when done to the required colour, serve immediately. Garnish to your personal preference.

Wine suggestion: White — "Preludio N.1" Castel del Monte DOC, Rivera (Chardonnay) or Red — "Elo Veni" Salento IGT, Leone de Castris (Negroamaro)

Monte Sant'Angelo

Monte Sant'Angelo is situated on a high, rugged Gargano spur that juts out over the Adriatic. It is reached by road from Manfredonia up steep, climbing zigzag hairpin turns that overlook a panorama of almost uninterrupted olive groves that form a dogtooth tapestry. It's a dramatic setting, although not the sole reason so many visitors come this far; the town is also home to the grotto of San Michele Arcangelo.

La Taverna Li Jalantuúmene
Gegé and Ninni Mangano

Piazza de Galganis, 5
71037 Monte Sant'Angelo
T: +39 0884 565 484
www.li-jalantuumene.it

Opening hours: 12.30–14.45;
  20.00–21.45
Closed: Tues
  (except Jun–Sept)
Holidays: Jan (all month)
Covers: 28 inside or 28 outside,
  but never both (Gegé decides
  because he's the owner!)

Primo: *orecchiette* with tomatoes. *Secondo* : sausages. To drink: one red wine (local) and water (still). When La Taverna Li Jalantuúmene opened in 1997 Gegé Mangano's menu had, indisputably, the virtue of brevity. And it was nothing if not consistent. For that was the complete, and unchanging menu. Day in, day out. For a year.

Today's diners, by contrast, can opt for soup of broad beans with porcini mushrooms and spices of the Gargano, pork cutlets beautifully presented with a vegetable garnish, saffron yoghurt with a semifreddo of chocolate and nuts, and much more, not to mention a stunning cheese selection and a wide choice of wines. A decade ago, however, Gegé's menu was still a work in progress or, as he less delicately puts it: "I started from nothing. I'd never been a chef."

But he knew what he wanted to do. "Most restaurants here have a tourist menu but I wanted to do something different." He asked all the applicants for the chef's post to suggest a menu. Every one of them came up with a list of dishes identical to all the other restaurants in town. "I thought it was crazy," he says. "It wasn't what I wanted my restaurant to be about. I'm for the three T's: *terra*, *tradizione* and *territorio*. They're very important to me, but I couldn't find a chef for my new restaurant willing to buy into that. So I told my wife Ninni that I'd work in the kitchen, and we'd start with a small menu."

Within his two dish limits, however, he could cook. "I'd say to new diners: "This is all I do, but I do it very well"." So well that he built up a fair following of regulars. And meanwhile he was learning. "Bit by bit, my repertoire expanded and I experimented," he says. "I went to great restaurants to eat. I looked at the food, at the wine. I started to go to the market in the morning to do my shopping."

Opposite
Top: Gegé Mangano, the head waiter who ably took over in the kitchen.

Bottom: Diners now have to make a choice from the menu.

So one year after his restaurant opened, his surprisingly loyal customers got a bit of a shock. Gegé announced: "There is now a menu of new dishes." Still, they soon got over it. As he explains: "By that time, everybody thought I was a bit bonkers so they expected unusual things to happen."

This wasn't the first time that Gegé was considered unhinged. There were a few raised eyebrows when he decided in his teens that he wanted to spend his life as a waiter. "It doesn't pay very well but the tips are good and you don't have to hang about for the money," he says. In time, however, it became more than just a source of income. "Everybody should wait tables at least once in their life," Gegé insists. "You learn to deal with the rich and the poor, the cultured and the non-cultured. Every day is a new lesson. I don't believe it's any old job; it's a big job."

And if you're going to do a big job properly you need to have the necessary skills, one of which, Gegé decided, was to speak English. Thus he kissed his tearful girlfriend Ninni goodbye and headed off to the Savoy in London. A good place to develop a new language? Not quite. Most of his workmates turned out to be from Napoli.

He still had a number of options. However, ignoring the most rational ones, Gegé went to the airport. The first domestic flight he saw on the departures board was for Newcastle — so that's where he went. "The people I met there were very warm and welcoming," he says. "They thought I was mad not to have gone to London or Cambridge, or somewhere like that, but I was very, very happy in Newcastle." But it wasn't his home and two years later he took his greatly improved waiting skills (and Geordie Italian-accented English) back to Monte Sant'Angelo and into the waiting arms of Ninni. And this time he stayed.

Still, Ninni was used to this sort of thing by now. Anna and Luigi (if we're being correct, but nobody ever calls the couple by their real names) met when she was ten and he was 11. Ninni was the most beautiful girl in town, while Gegé was, he insists, *brutto*. She loved him anyway, although he didn't make it easy. Once he had finished school he left town to find work. She was, for the first but not the last time, greatly distressed. But before he left he kissed her on the steps of an abandoned building that he said would one day house his restaurant. And he told her that he would come back, they would get married and they would have two children.

Which is pretty much how things turned out. He came back, they married, had children — and are still together after nearly 30 years. Oh, and the building came up for sale.

Except it wasn't quite that simple. At the time, there were no other restaurants in the historic centre of Monte Sant'Angelo. Consequently the pair waded through permit applications and a torrent of popular opinion telling them that it would never work.

Above left: Ninni who now heads up the dining room.

Above: *Ostie Ripiene,* wafers held together with caramelised almonds, a Monte Sant'Angelo speciality.

That was before the locals heard about the menu — and before the head waiter had to take over in the kitchen. Ninni, who had been responsible for organising the layout of the restaurant, now had to wait tables. It's just as well she likes talking to people. She doesn't, however, stop to chat with Gegé — at least during the working day. As Ninni puts it: "At home we are husband and wife. Here we work together like associates; we have to separate the roles."

Things have clearly changed a bit in ten years. The eccentricity remains, although it's Gegé's passion and sheer enthusiasm that you notice, and above all his food. Today he cooks dishes based on tradition, albeit with his own variations. Take a dessert he created. "I was eating a Sicilian *cannolo* and enjoying it," he says, "but I needed to link it with something of mine, something particular, something different." So he created a wine sauce based on *aleatico* — a grape used to make dessert wines. The result: *panacea di ricotta in salsa aleatica.* And he knows a bit about wine, by the way: he's proud to announce that in 1982 he was Italy's youngest sommelier.

He's proud of Puglia and specifically of his corner of it, the mountainous and thickly wooded Gargano peninsula, and is keen to introduce its merits to as wide an audience as possible (he dreams of opening a restaurant in Japan some

day). Even the oil you dip your fresh bread into is local. He strongly believes that all of us make connections between places and dishes, but particularly in Italy. "For me Italy is an association of products: if you say 'pasta' anywhere in the world people think of Italy, but say 'pizza' and they think of Naples. If you say Brunello, I think of Tuscany, Nero d'Avola I think of Sicily. *In Italia c'è un grande sforzo di associare il prodotto al territorio.* This is a great strength of Italy: to link the product with the region."

Which is why Gegé and Ninni are committed to doing their bit for the food of the Gargano. And that means that you now have to make a choice from the menu. As Gegé says, with some understatement: "We've come a long way in a decade from *orecchiette* and sausages."

Above left: A corner table on the first floor of the restaurant.

Above: Historic keys decorate a wall.

Medaglioni di Melanzane in Salsa di Pomodoro al Profumo di Basilico
Aubergine Medallions with Tomato and Basil Sauce

This is a great vegetable dish: a wonderful transformation of aubergines, tomatoes and stale bread.

SERVES 4

The sauce:
1 clove garlic
Extra virgin olive oil
500g tomatoes, skinned, deseeded and chopped
Small bunch basil, finely chopped
1 glass water

The medallions:
100g breadcrumbs made from stale bread
70g Pecorino, grated
3 eggs, beaten
1 clove garlic, chopped
Small bunch parsley, finely chopped
Salt and black pepper to taste
1 large +/-200g aubergine, cut widthways into ½ cm slices
Extra virgin olive oil

Make the sauce by frying the whole garlic clove in oil and remove once the oil is flavoured. Add the tomatoes, basil and the water to prevent burning. Leave on a gentle heat for 20 minutes.

In the meantime, mix the breadcrumbs, cheese, eggs, garlic, parsley, salt and pepper together in a bowl. Lay out half the aubergine slices, and spread ½cm of the paste on each slice. Top with a second aubergine slice and press down firmly. Heat up the oil and fry each medallion until they are cooked through and golden.

Gently place each medallion in the tomato sauce on a gentle heat. Turn the medallions over in the sauce so that they are fully coated, then serve them with extra sauce ladled over the top.

Wine suggestion: Rosé — "Vigna Mazzi" Salento IGT, Calò Rosa del Golfo (Negroamaro, Malvasia Nera)

Triangoli ai Porcini in Salsa di Noci
Triangular Mushroom Ravioli in a Walnut Sauce

This is one of Ninni's favourite dishes "because it's a little bit different and I love walnuts".

SERVES 4

Walnut sauce:
200g walnuts, shelled and chopped finely
Extra virgin olive oil
30g Parmesan
Pepper
¹/₂ clove garlic

Pasta:
375g "00" flour
125g semolina
Salt

3 eggs
1 spoon extra virgin olive oil
Water as needed

Ravioli filling:
200g porcini mushrooms, chopped
Extra virgin olive oil
1 garlic clove, finely chopped
500g fresh goat's ricotta, sieved
Small bunch parsley, finely chopped
Salt and pepper

Before making the walnut sauce, separate a small quantity of the walnuts for garnish. Then put the remainder and the other ingredients in a blender, with plenty of oil and when blitzed, keep to one side.

Make the filling by frying the mushrooms in the oil and garlic, and then mixing with the ricotta and parsley. Season to taste and leave to cool.

Make the pasta by mixing the flour, semolina and salt with the eggs. Add water and oil as needed. Work the dough until it becomes soft and elastic. With the use of a rolling pin and extra flour to prevent sticking, roll out 4 thin sheets. Cut into triangles, with a knife or pasta cutter and leave to rest for an hour.

Place a teaspoon of filling on the pasta and press closed with your fingers; eggs or milk will not be needed. Boil in plenty of salted boiling water, and drain when just al dente. Heat the walnut sauce in a frying pan and coat the ravioli lightly with the sauce on the heat. Serve immediately with a few chopped walnuts.

Wine suggestion: Red — Cacc'e Mmitte di Lucera DOC, Alberto Longo (Nero di Troia, Montepulciano, Bombino Bianco)

Orsara di Puglia

A small, remote medieval village, Orsara di Puglia is surrounded by gently rolling green hills and dramatic wind farms.Not many tourists make it this far but most of those who do pay a visit to Pane e Salute where excellent bread is still baked in an oven first used in 1526. The ancient oven retains heat exceptionally well, remaining warm a couple of days after the end of a baking session, which happens almost every three days when 50 huge loaves are baked in the oven. The loaves then make their way to many of the best restaurants throughout the province of Foggia.

Peppe Zullo Peppe Zullo

Piano Paradiso
71027 Orsara di Puglia
Tel: +39 0881 964 763
www.peppezullo.it

Opening hours: 12.30–15.30;
  evenings only with reservation
Closed: Tues
Holidays: Nov (all month)
Covers: 30

It's pointless to resist Peppe Zullo's enthusiasm for nature. In fact it's pointless to resist his enthusiasm for anything. Herbs, America, cheese, local community, wine, bread — but mainly nature, from his own backyard, with as few adornments as possible. Or, as he puts it, "natural gifts. If nature gives us something so good, so healthy, why as a chef not use them? Why would I want to use industrial food? Why in Orsara would I want to use steak from Argentina? Or lamb from New Zealand? Why would people want to come here and eat these things?"

Orsara di Puglia, Peppe's home town and that of his family for at least three generations, is in the north of the region, an area he describes as "the California of Italy, big with a plain, hills and wind farms". Orsara is also home to his restaurant. He bought some land on the spot where as a boy he played football with his friends ("I wasn't that good"), built a house and then opened a restaurant on its ground floor.

Word spread quickly. People decided it was where they wanted to celebrate important events: weddings, Communions, christenings. With only room for 20 diners, the restaurant couldn't cope. The result was a venue next door for larger functions: Nuova Sala Paradiso. It offers the same food (after all, that's what they came for) but has a capacity of 150.

The restaurant is still doing well despite only being open without a reservation at lunchtime. That suits the needs of a clientele that is not, in the main, from the local village; it is, to put it mildly, not the easiest of drives after dark.

It's worth the trip of course. You may even be seated with a view into the open kitchen and get to see the menu being prepared. It's a constantly changing, seasonal menu, and by no means a vast one. "It's common sense," says Peppe. "If

you want to offer freshly prepared, seasonal food you can't have a choice of 40 dishes." Let alone dishes whose ingredients have such a strong local flavour. Take the *passata,* for example. "We get through about 10,000 litres of *passata* a year made from 15,000 kilos of tomatoes, and I grow about 8,000 of those," says Peppe. The others come from small gardens around Orsara because Peppe prefers to buy from people who live locally. In his words, "it's a good philosophy".

And that philosophy extends to his beloved Villa Jamele, a short distance from the restaurant, in the grounds of which he cultivates his produce and rears his livestock. A big yellow villa that provides both overnight accommodation and a large professional kitchen for his cooking classes, it already has school groups turning up. "They get really excited about picking things," says Peppe. "It's so much better than just playing computer games."

They are not the only excited ones. Peppe's eyes light up when he tells you about the wild herbs — *melissa, sivoni, puleo* — growing wherever they can take root. He eulogises about the different colours, smells and tastes, and walking through the fields you can see, smell, almost feel the dizzying proof of his enthusiasm.

It comes as no surprise to learn that he is an organic grower. There is automatic irrigation but water is all he adds. "All plants were once wild," he says. "The wild peas growing at the edge of this land are small but delicious."

He is also particularly proud of his orchard, which has about 25 different types of apple tree, most of them ancient varieties that he is trying to keep going. If you look closely you can see some fine examples of grafting, the work of a local man. He's in his 80s but still pops by once a week to check on progress.

That's the sort of effect Peppe has on people. He has an innate flair for enthusing others — like the friend who is a highly regarded cheese maker. He has, inevitably, got involved in Peppe's cheese production.

Peppe is (unsurprisingly) convinced that people don't understand how to make good cheese any longer. "Cheese is the land," he says. "An animal's milk tastes of the natural herbs that it eats, so there's a very strong link between cheese and *territorio*." He also much prefers aged cheese because the process is more complicated. "It's like making wine; you have to think how long it's going to last. It's much more challenging."

And, yes, he produces wine too. Called Ursaria, which was the ancient name of Orsara, it's a red blend of two or three grapes, depending on the year, from Ducanese, Uva di Troia, Merlot and Cabernet Sauvignon. This is no hobby, incidentally. Peppe's father used to have a small vineyard and Peppe somehow found time to become a sommelier. This is wine for the restaurant.

And the restaurant is a story in itself — or at least how he got into the business. You certainly wouldn't have expected it when, at the age of 20, he decided to

move to the US. But even then he dreamed of running a restaurant. However, he had to settle for saving up his pay as a mechanic until in 1978 he opened Peppe's Buongustaio. He ran that in Boston for three years. A dream come true? Not exactly. He explains that it was harder then than it would be now "because at that time Italian cooking in the States was an Italian-American hybrid. The known and expected dishes were meatballs, cannelloni, lasagne and pizza."

So back to Orsara and real Italian food? Not quite. There were stints in Vegas, LA and Mexico first. But travel undoubtedly broadened Peppe's mind: it made him appreciate the virtues of what is on his doorstep. As he says: "So many people have stopped respecting their *territorio*. Nature gives us herbs, fruit, vegetables and if we don't pick them, use them and eat them, we'll lose them. I cook seasonally and I'll develop new recipes, but the longer I spend cooking the more I like the natural approach. I want to keep my recipes simple without changing the natural flavours."

And, his customers will no doubt tell you, that's exactly what he does. His favourite dish is fresh pasta, cooked simply with seasonal vegetables and herbs. But the rest of the menu offers an equally captivating selection of the simple and the delicious. Try the wild vegetables, maybe asparagus, with Peppe's own olive oil

Above left: The enthusiastic Peppe Zullo.

Above: Peppe, who is also a sommelier, produces his own wine called Ursaria.

and local wild herbs. Or vermicelli with artichokes. Or *millefoglie* of wild boar with borage. Or wood-roasted Orsara lamb with wild thyme and grilled potatoes. As he says: "From good, simple things, you can make great things."

He adores Pugliese cooking and won't use butter or cream "because they don't belong here. I only use extra virgin olive oil." This view even extends to implements. "Flavours are ruined, they're killed, by gadgets and mechanical appliances," he says, "whereas using basic implements gives your hands a connection with the food, and our hands are treasures. *Le nostre mani sono un tesoro.*"

Yes, it really is pointless to resist Peppe Zullo's enthusiasms. And why would you want to? However, there is one thing that can stop him in his tracks. Going out in the early morning to pick the day's produce with Peppe is a surprisingly calming experience. Out in his fields, the sun floods down with a strong, welcome breeze and you can hear in the background the sound of village church bells, roosters and tractors. The occasional rotor blade of a wind turbine peeks from between the hills and, for once, Peppe is lost for words. Communing with his plants, at one with Mother Nature.

Wood-roasted meat with wild herbs, a fine example of Peppe's belief that "from good simple things you can make great things."

Insalata di Fave e Cacioricotta al Profumo di Menta
Broad Bean and Cacioricotta Salad with Mint

This dish combines two of Peppe's favourite ingredients: fresh vegetables and cheese. Vincotto is cooked grape must which is reduced until it becomes very thick. Peppe suggests using Balsamic vinegar as an alternative explaining that "vincotto is made more quickly than good Balsamic vinegar". If you're not using freshly picked broad beans, you may want to blanch and double pod them, and increase the quantity accordingly .

SERVES 4

300g fresh broad beans	**Mint**
200g Cacioricotta (or fresh goat's cheese, preferably unsalted)	**Extra virgin olive oil**
	Vincotto (or good Balsamic vinegar)

Pod the beans. Cut the cheese into small pieces, approximately the same size as the beans. Make a dressing of finely chopped mint and oil and dress the beans and cheese. Put a drizzle of Vincotto around the edge of the plate. Decorate with mint and serve.

Wine suggestion: White — "Briciole" Salento IGT, Azienda Monaci (Chardonnay, Sauvignon)

Funghi Cardoncelli al Forno con Crostoncini in Salsa di Marasciuolo

Oven Baked Cardoncelli Mushrooms with Marasciuolo Toasts

Peppe grows marasciuolo and explains that "it is a brassica and has a gentle garlic flavour". This is evident when the leaves are smelt, even before they are tasted.

SERVES 4

300g cardoncelli mushrooms
Extra virgin olive oil
Sea salt

200g marasciuolo tops
(or blanched sprouting broccoli
with garlic to taste)
4 slices Pugliese bread or another
bread made with hard wheat flour

Brush the mushrooms clean, but don't wash them. Put in an oven dish with some olive oil and place in a preheated 200°C oven for 15–20 minutes. The mushrooms should become golden and lightly crispy on the outside.

In the meantime, wash and chop the marasciuolo tops. Put in a bowl with lots of olive oil and marinade for at least 10–15 minutes, or even refrigerate and use the following day.

Cut each slice of bread into two, and put in the oven for a few minutes to warm through and so that the cut sides of the bread become slightly crispy without becoming golden. Spoon the marasciuolo on top of the bread and serve with a generous spoonful of mushrooms.

Wine suggestion: Rosé — "Donnadele" Puglia IGT, Alberto Longo (Negroamaro)

Polignano a Mare

Polignano a Mare is a distinctive town rising up from the sea (Polignano means 'built high') with medieval streets cascading down to its grottoes. Despite its quiet, languid daytime feel, its community atmosphere becomes spirited at around seven in the evening when everybody seems to come out to play.

You may be surprised to see Brazilian flags draped from balconies and windows during international football contests. There is, however, a strong link between the town and Brazil; apparently, the Polignano dialect can regularly be heard in some quarters of São Paulo.

Da Tuccino Pasquale Centrone

via S. Caterina 69/F
70044 Polignano a Mare
T: +39 080 4241 560
www.tuccino.it

Opening hours: 12.30–15.00;
  20.00–23.30 (winter) and
  20.00–24.00 (summer)
Closed: Mon (and Sun
  evening in the winter)
Holidays: 30 Nov–31 Jan
Covers: 70 inside;100 outside

"You're the man!" The emphatic cry from a wine bar owner would probably be a bit shocking if it was unexpected. So far, however, during a five-minute detour through Polignano with Pasquale Centrone 99 per cent of the people we've seen have wanted to greet or chat with him.

Why is Pasquale so popular? Or at least so well known? Is it simply that his family hails from Polignano? Or is it that he runs a restaurant acclaimed in the area (and well beyond) for its raw fish? Let's see...

Da Tuccino, a couple of kilometres outside Polignano on the seafront, was set up by Pasquale's father almost by accident. When Vito Centrone was 17 his own father died and so, to help support his family, he began work, mainly selling produce. But his passion was the sea — one of his many jobs at that time was as a fisherman — and after a few years he concentrated on trading seafood such as mussels and oysters. Then he started mixing *acqua dolce*, the fresh water from the mountains, with seawater. The result was larger and tastier mussels.

His reputation soon spread. By now he no longer just sold fish for people to take away, but also for them to eat on the spot from his seaside shack. Sophisticated it was not: long tables, plates of mussels with beer, bread and Provolone cheese. Other shellfish were added along with spaghetti and rice dishes. When more help was needed with the cooking his wife, Pasquale's mother, was roped in. She wasn't keen at first but gave it a go and eventually decided she liked it, which may explain why she was still helping 50 years later. And even though she stepped away from the hob many years ago, she's still a presence at the restaurant, quietly sitting in the corner where long-standing regulars step by to check on her wellbeing.

Opposite: Pasquale really knows his fish, and, more importantly, the fish sellers up and down both the Adriatic and Ionian coasts know that he knows.

It's no surprise then that, as Pasquale says: "I knew that my destiny was to be in this restaurant." His father, however, insisted he get an education first. He did — and it wasn't just academic. "I began to introduce new wines, new products, a new way of eating. Raw fish: scampi, prawns, fish carpaccio. Why? Because in my trips around, and I'd travelled a lot, I'd looked at other restaurants, and what they were doing, and thought if they're doing this, and they don't have the great fish that we have, then I want to do it better."

He also moved the business to bigger premises but, he says, "we still keep it simple...good fresh produce, served with whatever you want. Our shoots of radish, or rocket or alfalfa are top quality but our side dishes are not 'studied' or affected; they're served as at home."

Home is more than just a reference: it's his inspiration. "The first thing we Italians do is to eat well at home," he says. "Why are our mothers great cooks? Because they know how to shop well. They negotiate with strength at the market and they know how to recognise good fresh produce. Which means they know how to cook because that's the basis of everything. You can be the greatest chef but if you don't have good produce your dishes will never be great dishes." That, you soon realise, applies to Pasquale too. "What we offer is based on good shop-

ping. *Il mio compito principale è di essere bravo nell'acquistare.* My job is to be a good shopper."

The fresh fish display is impressive and inspires animated discussions.

And he is. Pasquale really knows his fish, and, more importantly, the fish sellers up and down both the Adriatic and Ionian coasts know that he knows. It's all down to experience, he explains. "You need to frequent the places where people live with fish. There's no technique; it's not something that can be taught, but after a while you can tell from which sea they've come, how deep the water was, if they've been freshly caught. Even with scampi you learn to tell whether they've just been caught or are a few days old." And don't take his word for it: ask the fish dealers at the market. "I'm very thorough and meticulous. They know that. I've bought a basket of live scampi thinking that they're all good, then got them home and discovered that they're all small at the bottom. But you make that mistake once and you don't make the same mistake again."

He especially likes big fish, not least because they make a better impression on his fish bench. "Words written on a menu are one thing, but there's nothing like going to the fish bench to see what's on offer and really feeling enthusiastic about what you're going to eat. I never go to the market knowing what I'm going to buy. I go, have a look around and buy what I fall in love with."

And so do the customers. "When they're put out on the bench here, the big fishes have intense colour, the grey, the blue, the gold," Pasquale says. "When these fish are fresh you put them with vegetables and they shine, everything shines. The moment customers come to the bench they want to buy everything and that's the effect that makes me happy. A menu doesn't have the same effect." The quality of the fare at Da Tuccino means that it's not cheap, but the locals who return regularly clearly feel that it's worth it.

The display of fresh fish at Da Tuccino is certainly impressive; in fact it's pure theatre. There's the tableau itself of course, but there are also the animated Italians gathered round discussing what to choose, ringmaster Pasquale jumping in to dispense advice (and not just on fish), and Franco, who has been cleaning fish here for 30 years, deftly scaling, trimming and filleting. You could sell tickets for this.

However, as you will have guessed by now, Da Tuccino's main draw is not just the fish, but a very specific way of presenting it: *crudo* — raw — a Baresi tradition that is being rediscovered by diners all over the world.

If you can't bear the idea of eating raw fish, or if you're worried about your constitution being able to take it, Pasquale says, "everything that we serve raw, we'll prepare cooked for you". But if you try it, you may be surprised. "Often foreigners sit down here and stress that they don't want raw fish," says Pasquale. "But then they try a small piece as an experiment, and they're amazed that they enjoy it so much." It's all part of the Da Tuccino experience, after all. "Once people look at the fish display," says Pasquale, "well, at that point they're involved in the adventure."

But Pasquale won't force the issue; he and his team just want you to enjoy yourself. So is the customer always right? "It's not a matter of being right," he insists. "It's simply whatever people like, whatever makes them happy. For instance, the great sommeliers advise against eating fish with red wine, because red is more aggressive, richer in tannins and will cover the palate; but if you want red wine with your fish then that's right for you. It's not for me to change people's minds and ruin their fun."

And fun is what the buzz of Sunday lunchtime at Da Tuccino is about. Large multigenerational family tables smile at couples. Are they on their first date? Whatever the guessing, it won't be done in hushed tones; questions will be asked directly by the end of the antipasto at the latest. Grandparents help toddlers to come to grips with what's on their plates. Teenagers teach their younger siblings all that they know about different types of raw squid. Look out to sea meanwhile and the view is a panorama of Italians at play: serious bronzing and posing, pedaloes, swimming races, I'm-successful boats, splashing and yelping.

The evening is slightly different. That's when the roof opens. "That's why we don't need aircon in the summer," says Pasquale, "because most people eat in the

Opposite
Top: Antonella, Pasquale's wife helps out and charmingly greets diners.

Bottom: The Da Tuccino dining room overlooks the sea.

evening, and it's cooler and they're outside. In the evening, when everything is opened up, even if it's hot, we're beneath the stars."

Day or night, Pasquale and his wife Antonella are there to greet everyone and help Damiano and the busy team of waiters. It's a large restaurant but the staff give it a huge amount of soul and personal feel. As Pasquale puts it: "I constantly tell my boys, the waiters, to always try to talk to people."

It's a team effort all right — and possibly more than that. As Pasquale says: "The cook has worked with us for 30 years; the second cook has been with us for 20 years. Many waiters have been with us for 20, 21, 18 years. There's always been a family atmosphere here."

Speaking of families, would Pasquale like one of his children to take over Da Tuccino when the time is right? "Of course," is the answer. He's keen to point out that each of his daughters is *brava*. "If one of the girls becomes a restaurateur, that's fine." But Vito, his son, is the eldest, and even though he's barely entered his teens, he comes to the market, he knows the fish — sometimes he even goes to the fish bench and serves there — and he loves *crudo*. He even knows the wine. Well, he wets his lips — but he can still identify a 14º negroamaro. At the moment though, Vito's plans are to become an engineer. "Unbelievable," says Pasquale. "How many engineers does the world need?"

Still, Pasquale would be a hard act to follow. He describes himself as "somebody who's always on the go, who never stops — a *trottola*". *Trottola* means spinning top. It's certainly apt. His van draws up outside the restaurant from the fish market and he toots his horn so that it can be unloaded immediately, before he whirls off to the next market, travelling to both Adriatic and Ionian ports and clocking up hundreds of kilometres daily. But Pasquale combines energy with informality. For all that the waiting staff are decked out in smart, old-school attire, Pasquale takes the casual, and often very brightly coloured option, which reflects the fact that for all the linen tablecloths and napkins this is a comfortable, relaxed place where the customers leave looking happier than when they arrived.

So what, in a nutshell, is the secret of Pasquale's success? "The primary produce; that's always it," he says. "The research and the primary produce. And the welcome."

And Pasquale himself, you can't help but think. Back on the streets of Polignano, our five-minute diversion through town turns into a two-hour detour featuring introductions to numerous cousins, amazing coffee from one of his uncles, and a bottle of *prosecco* with a friend. The timetable may go down the gurgler, but it's fantastic entertainment. He is the man.

Clockwise from top left:
Pasquale meticulously checking produce at Gallipoli market.

The fish counter at Da Tuccino.

Pasquale catching up with some regulars.

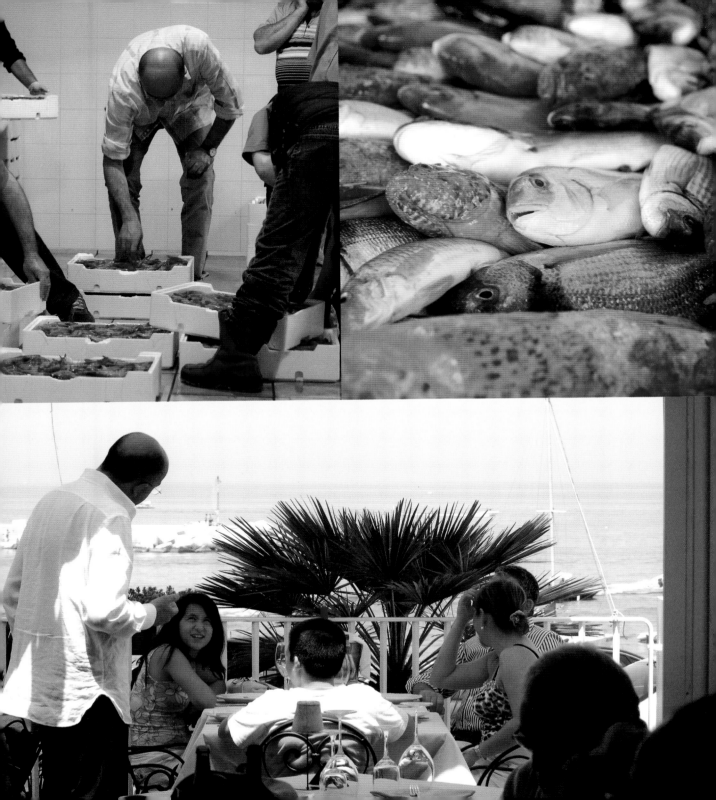

Orecchiette Nere alle Vongole e Fiori di Zucchina
Black Orecchiette with Clams and Courgette Flowers

Pasquale's personal preference is for dried rather than fresh pasta. "Those of us who have a palate and sense of taste formed by what was eaten many years ago prefer dried pasta. You have to watch fresh pasta very closely otherwise it becomes too soft, unlike pasta made with very hard grain. Tastes and ideas change all the time, but for me, the use of fresh pasta is sometimes contrary."

SERVES 4

Extra virgin olive oil
1 shallot, chopped
150g courgettes
Handful courgette flowers
400g clams, washed thoroughly
White wine
300g small prawns, shelled

200g cherry tomatoes, halved
Salt and pepper
400g black squid ink orecchiette

In a pan, heat the oil and fry the shallot. Cut the courgettes and flowers into julienne strips and add all the courgettes and half the flowers to the pan. Add the clams in their shells with a splash of white wine. Keep on the heat to let the clams open and the liquid evaporate. Add the prawns and the tomatoes, adjust the seasoning and leave to cook gently.

Boil the orecchiette in salted water. Sauté everything together in the pan and serve with the remaining raw courgette flowers.

Wine suggestion: Rosé — Rosa del Golfo Salento IGT, Calò Rosa del Golfo (Negroamaro, Malvasia Nera)

Spigola con Patate al Profumo di Timo al Limone
Sea Bass with Lemon Thyme Potatoes

Although crudo, raw fish, are Pasquale's favourite, he likes the simplicity of this recipe because "it makes my palate happy".

SERVES 4

Extra virgin olive oil
1kg sea bass, scaled and cleaned
Salt and pepper

800g potatoes, peeled and thinly sliced, blanched and cooled
Lemon thyme, finely chopped

Preheat the oven to 200°C. Grease an ovenproof dish with olive oil. Season the sea bass. In a bowl, coat the potato slices lightly with olive oil, salt, pepper and lemon thyme. Place a few potato slices in the bottom of the dish and lay the sea bass on top. Cover the fish with the potato slices, slightly overlapping them like fish scales.

Cook in the oven for about 35 minutes, until the potatoes are cooked and golden and the fish is cooked through.

Wine suggestion: White — "Placeo" Salento IGT, Cardone (Chardonnay)

Trani

Prosperous Trani has a picture postcard port used both by leisure craft and working fishing boats. In fact if you happen to be enjoying a harbourside cappuccino at the right time of day, you may be entertained by heated discussions between returning fishermen and potential buyers.

Trani's iconic cathedral next to the sea sits at the foot of a long jetty which curves round, affording good views back to the town. Stroll out along here during the summer siesta, join the locals taking the sun on the rocks before returning to work and watch the young and beautiful (and less so) relax by sunbathing or jumping blithely into the sea

Osteria Corteinfiore Michele Matera

via Ognissanti 18
70059 Trani
T: +39 0883 50 84 02
www.corteinfiore.it

Opening hours: 12.30–14.00;
 20.00–23.00
Closed: Sun evening and Mon
Holidays: Jan (all month)
Covers: 70 winter; 80 summer

Michele Matera began his culinary career in a nightclub where he was in charge of the snack food. The first time he flipped a burger it stuck to the ceiling. Nowadays he prefers fish — raw, simply prepared fish. And he doesn't miss the burgers at all. "If you were to eat nothing but meat for six months, you'd be begging to stop," he says, "but I've never heard anybody want to stop eating fish. It's just so good. Fish eaters never have any problems in life."

Just as well fish is his business. He clearly loves the stuff — almost as much as he loves the sea, especially when he's sailing on it. In fact if he could change just one thing about his restaurant, Osteria Corteinfiore, he says, "I'd like it to be nearer to the sea. Well, on the sea."

Still, even when he's not on the ocean wave, Michele is not far from it. He spends every morning at various fish markets along the coast. Why not buy everything from the Trani port? It is on his doorstep, after all. "Because every fish market has its own specialities," he says. "Trani has very good fish but I buy my sea bass from Manfredonia or Bari and the best scampi come from Molfetta."

He knows his scampi all right. That's why it's the most popular *secondo* by far at Osteria Corteinfiore. Simply steamed and served with lemon and excellent olive oil, it's a light and delicious way to follow an antipasto fish selection.

Michele speaks with authority about buying and preparing fish — but his insight goes well beyond the market and the kitchen. Having spent his career in hospitality, he knows that when people go out to eat they don't just want excellent food, but a warm welcome and an enjoyable place in which to relax. And that's exactly what they get at his restaurant, as you'll find out when he greets you and talks you through the menu and the day's specials.

Clockwise from top left:
Michele Matera outside the entrance to Osteria Corteinfiore.

Diners sharing the lunchtime antipasto selection.

The interior is warm and friendly.

In summer the garden is a tranquil oasis of fragrant shrubs and shady trees.

Turn up often enough and you may even become a friend. Over the years, he's become friends with all of his regulars — and there are more than a few of them, many travelling from Lecce, Foggia or even Napoli. He wants to know the story of every table. "*Ogni tavola ha una storia diversa,*" he says gleefully.

He's a bit of a charmer, our Michele — but it's not just schmoozing, he insists; this is what southern Italians are really like. "We're Latin people here: we listen to Latin music — *salsa merengue* — we have 'molto easy' souls," he says. "We're very open and all friends of each others' friends. I really enjoy the whole "Ciao! Ciao!" giving everybody a kiss and finding out how people are."

The warm, friendly interior is in sharp contrast to the apparently self-effacing exterior. In fact from the outside it's not obvious that Corteinfiore is a restaurant: when closed, the large wooden doors could mask the entrance to any manner of enterprise. The garden therefore is a complete surprise.

Which is just what Michele wanted. For many years, his ambition was to set up his own restaurant with a secluded outside eating area away from car fumes and noisy streets. He'd been working in Trani for many years when his search yielded an excellent result: a palazzo just a few metres from the port featuring a garden which had been abandoned for 60 years. Perfect.

From the outside, it's not obvious that Osteria Corteinfiore is a restaurant; when closed the large wooden doors could mask the entrance to any manner of enterprise.

The palazzo originally had a garden on each of its three levels, but only the one on the ground floor remained. It's been cleaned up and now houses a series of patios, the main one of which is enclosed and heated in the winter. In the summer it's a tranquil oasis of fragrant shrubs and shady trees, which is transformed into a magically lit sanctuary in the evenings, enticing both local and visiting romantics to experience Michele's excellent food and warm welcome.

Not surprisingly, Michele's parents are proud of his achievement; more than that, they are a part of it. His father, Francesco, does the daily shopping and his mother, Maria, prepares an extensive array of desserts. Meanwhile, his wife and his brother help out and play a big part in organising promotions. The promotions must be working because in the summer Michele has no spare time, even for his beloved sailing. All is put right during his month's holiday in January, however, when he and his wife treat themselves to a sailing trip. It's too cold to sail locally but then there's always the Caribbean. Problem very nicely solved.

And when he returns it's all hands on deck again at Osteria Corteinfiore. But with so many family members involved, is there ever confusion over who runs the show? "Not at all," says Michele firmly. "I make all the decisions. If everybody is a captain, a boat doesn't sail – it sinks!" And he should know.

Above left: The day's specials being prepared.

Above: Maria, Michele's mother, prepares the desserts.

Pesce Spada Marinato all'Arancia con Trancio di Filetto di Tonno alla Brace

Orange Marinated Swordfish with Grilled Tuna

This light dish is perfect for hot summer days and the kick in the dressing is a good contrast with the fish.

SERVES 4

16 slices fresh swordfish
1 litre freshly squeezed orange juice
1 small bunch fresh oregano
1 tablespoon salted capers

1 small mild chilli
Extra virgin olive oil
200g tuna cut into 4 cubes

Marinate the swordfish in the orange juice for 24 hours.

Blend the oregano, capers, chilli and olive oil together to make a dressing.

Drain the swordfish from the marinade, arrange on a serving platter and drizzle over some extra virgin olive oil. Heat the grill to high and lightly oil the tuna. Quickly grill the tuna cuts on both sides to sear the outside, leaving the inside rare.

Place the tuna in the centre of the plate and drizzle with the dressing to taste.

Wine suggestion: White — "Pietra Bianca" Castel del Monte DOC, Tormaresca (Chardonnay, Fiano)

Tagliolini con Vongole Veraci, Coda di Rospo e Basilico
Tagliolini with Palourdes, Monkfish and Basil

Michele uses the larger and tastier palourdes or carpet shell clams for this dish.

SERVES 4
320g tagliolini
1 clove garlic, peeled and left whole
Extra virgin olive oil
200g monkfish, cut into small pieces
10 cherry tomatoes, quartered
200g clams
Small bunch basil

Cook the pasta in plenty of boiling, salted water until just al dente, drain and keep to one side. In the meantime, fry the garlic in the oil to flavour it and then discard. Add the monkfish, the tomatoes and the clams and cook until the fish is lightly browned and the clams have opened. Add the pasta and sauté, then add the basil leaves. Serve immediately on a heated plate.

Wine suggestion: White — "Teresa Manara", Salento IGT, Cantele (Chardonnay)

Torrente Antico Savino and Sara Pasquadibisceglie

via Eduardo Fusco 3
70059 Trani
T: +39 0883 48 79 11

Opening hours: 12.30–14.45;
  20.00–23.30
Closed: Sun evening and Mon
Holidays: 10–30 Jan
Covers: 30

Wine bottles. Everywhere. A vast, almost riotous selection of wine bottles ranging from the very gluggable to the very, very expensive. And that's before you get so much as a glimpse of the wine cellar. Let's face it: as soon as you enter Torrente Antico, you realise that wine is important.

When Savino Pasquadibisceglie and his wife Sara found the building that now houses their restaurant, the cellar was, for them, a big attraction. But there wasn't a lot of competition for number 3, via Eduardo Fusco. It's a small road in the historic centre of Trani and closed off to traffic. There's hardly any passing trade. Still, that suited Sara and Savino; they wanted somewhere quiet with only a few covers to enable them to do things properly. And after that? "We've just relied on word of mouth," says Sara. "People who enjoy our food tell others." So, in 1990, having thoroughly cleaned the cellar (and sorted out a few humidity problems), they stocked it in style and Torrente Antico opened for business.

Savino's parents were teachers but, from the age of 11, he was allowed to help out in a professional kitchen after school. He had been in the business for well over 20 years when he acquired the premises that now house Torrente Antico — more than enough time to decide what he wanted to do with his own restaurant. Savino chose to concentrate on "traditional but innovative cooking". The results, it has to be said, are utterly delicious: dishes that show his deep understanding of flavours. Dishes like the sumptuous (and beautifully presented) grilled prawns on a potato cake with leaves in a balsamic dressing. Or the traditional 'Benedetto' lamb with (incredibly sweet) baby peas and scrambled egg. Or the linguine with courgettes, clams and the freshness of mint. Not to mention an irresistible caramel *panna cotta*.

One of Savino's pleasures is really good wine.

And the subtlety and substance of Savino's food are both reflected in Sara's service. She looks after the front of house with Dino, who has been with the couple since the early days. True professionals, both of them (just watch Dino as he heads, tails and fillets your fish at the table perfectly and in seconds), but always friendly.

Sara enjoys working with Savino, not least because it means she gets to see him. For the first ten years of their marriage they barely met; he left before she awoke and returned very late. "For 36 years," he says, "I've had no more than five hours sleep a night."

And she enjoys the company beyond the kitchen too. The regulars are clearly fond of Sara and she of them, playfully (and hoarsely) confiding that she's partly lost her voice and so can't tell Savino off, something she usually attempts when he goes on one of his shopping sprees. Every so often they'll agree that he has done enough shopping and a moratorium is due; it doesn't last. Sara knows that he has a stubborn streak and just can't stop buying stock for the restaurant, insisting that "the larder should always be full". He doesn't believe in freezers in any case. It's the same with the wine cellar. Yes, he'll agree: there's enough wine. Then another couple of cases arrive.

Savino and Sara outside the entrance to Torrente Antico.

Freshly delivered fish awaiting Savino.

Although his bottle shopping covers the full extent of Puglia, and much of the rest of the world, the produce in his kitchen is local: fish from Trani and Barletta, vegetables from the Valle d'Itria. Well, there is an exception, although it's hard to blame him for it: in winter he makes full use of white Alba truffles.

Being born and bred in such a beautiful port, is he a huge fish fan? "I love fish," he admits, "especially in spring and summer. I really enjoy it raw. Red mullet, filleted and marinated with olive oil, lemon, salt and pepper. That's all you need. Delicious."

But when all is said and done, Savino's preference is meat, especially in winter, a season he prefers because the colder months usher in hearty soups and rib-sticking roasts — all of them great accompaniments to the gutsy red wines he so adores.

For someone who is still in his home town, Savino has a reputation that stretches well beyond it: everybody in Puglia knows, or knows of him. The verdict, incidentally, is unanimous: he's a lovely bloke, but completely mad. And endearingly enthusiastic. In the same way that he appreciates straightforward Negroamaro at Eur 15 as well as Sassicaia and Chateau Margaux, he has fun with all types of music. Pavarotti, Hard-Fi, Verdi, Snow Patrol: he'll dance around the kitchen and the restaurant to any of them. When it's closed, luckily.

It's not just food, wine and music, either. With his first ever wage packet, Savino bought a motorbike, and he still can't resist spending money once or twice a year on two and, increasingly, four-wheeled vehicles. Then there's his weakness for watches (although at least it means he has a reputation for punctuality). Of course, all that shopping can take it out of you so he likes to escape to the pool — the pool table, that is. Many chefs take a nap between lunch and dinner service, but not Savino. His distraction is to play billiards for two or three hours, then return to the restaurant and prep for dinner.

Sara is the perfect foil to his quirkiness. Savino's been known to get into trouble as he always speaks his mind. She, on the other hand, would have done well in the diplomatic corps.

However, they both love their customers. Sara is, naturally, more elegant in her praise, describing the diners who come to Torrente Antico as "intelligent and civilised". Savino simply says: "I have respect for those at my table," but that says a lot. He loves good food and he wants the diners in his restaurant to enjoy every mouthful of what he serves. Which is why he states matter-of-factly that "*io metto tutto per fare un buon piatto*. I'll do everything I can to serve a good plate of food." Hence if all you fancy is simple spaghetti and olive oil, he'll give you that with pleasure — and lots of it. He is, says Sara, "generous of heart and generous with his servings".

Most customers, on arriving, take a wander around to inspect any newly acquired bottles, ask a few questions about wines they haven't seen before, and keep some potential orders in mind to accompany their meal. Giovanni is one such, a regular who frequently does a 90-kilometre round trip from Matera (over the Basilicata border) for lunch. He thinks Savino's food is "the best. But...." But what? "But he is completely mad. Nobody in their right mind would keep that number of bottles in a restaurant cellar." Even madder, Torrente Antico is reputedly the only restaurant in Puglia without a wine list. Still, says Savino, it's better to have the wine and not the list, rather than a fancy list, but not the right wine when you want it. "It's important to enjoy the things you like in life, and one of my pleasures is really good wine," he says.

So how many bottles are there Savino? "I have absolutely no idea," he says, laughing. "7,000? 8,000? Does it matter?"

Soufflé di Patate, Asparagi e Scampi
Potato, Asparagus and Langoustine Soufflé

Savino insists that it is absolutely critical to have excellent fish stock for this dish.
He recommends using leftovers from fish which are particularly full of flavour and
to filter the stock before using.

SERVES 4

450g potatoes	Handful parsley, chopped
100g asparagus	50cl double cream
Extra virgin olive oil	2 egg whites, whipped to soft peak
4 langoustines, shelled	stage
100cl top quality fish stock	Garnish: 8 langoustines and a few
Salt and pepper to taste	clams

Boil the potatoes, whole and unpeeled, on a gentle heat. Peel and mash to a very smooth paste. Boil or steam the asparagus and cool down rapidly with iced water.

In another pan, put the oil, the shelled langoustines and the drained asparagus and cook lightly on a high heat, adding a ladle of the stock. Cook gently for 5 minutes and leave to cool before roughly crushing and then mixing together with the mashed potatoes. Add salt, pepper, parsley and cream and combine evenly before mixing in the egg whites.

Divide between 4 largish well-greased metal moulds and cook in a pre-heated 170°C oven for 15 minutes. When the soufflés are set and golden (but remain soft), put in the centre of the serving plate and remove the mould. Cook the clams and the langoustines on a high heat for a garnish and serve with a little warmed fish stock.

Wine suggestion: White — Sauvignon de la Tour DOC, Villa Russiz (Sauvignon Blanc)

Soufflé al Cioccolato
Chocolate Fondant

This is a chocolate dessert that remains runny in the centre, hence the need to serve it immediately it is taken from the oven. For that reason, the serving plates should be prepared with fruit or your preferred garnish ready for immediate plating up.

SERVES 4

100g good quality chocolate
  (72% cocoa)
100g butter
3 eggs
3 egg yolks

100g self-raising flour
100g caster sugar
Seasonal fruit, cream or ice cream as
  preferred, to serve

Gently melt the chocolate and butter together in a bowl over a simmering pan of water, taking care that the bottom of the bowl does not touch the water. In a separate bowl, beat together the eggs, egg yolks, flour and sugar. Mix everything together and spoon into greased and floured moulds; fill to 3mm from the top.

Cook in a preheated oven at 200°C for about 9 minutes. Remove carefully from moulds onto prepared plates and serve quickly while still hot.

Wine suggestion: Dessert — Banyuls Hors d'Age AOC, Domaine de Valcros (Grenache)

Regional Specialities

Puglia is known as the *orto*, or vegetable garden, of Italy. It's easy to see why.
Its relative flatness, good soil and climate make it ideal for cultivation, and
wheat, vegetables, fruit and nuts thrive. There are thus abundant regional
specialities: excellent breads and *taralli*; pasta, especially *orecchiette*,
the 'little ears'; olive oil and *olive di Cerignola*; a wide range of cheeses;
carob; fish; meat products including the antipasto favourite *capocollo*;
lampascioni, the bulbs that resemble bitter onions; *latte di mandorla*,
the local almond milk that is drunk diluted with water; and Puglia's
wines, whose reputation, both national and international, is growing.

Many Pugliese food producers are small, but the quality of their produce means it sells not only throughout the region but elsewhere in Italy — and increasingly abroad. That is because, even though some are well-established family firms, there is no resting on laurels. The younger generations of these families are keen to innovate and improve. But they are still, and proudly, Pugliese businesses. Here are some of them.

Caseificio Masi: Cheese

Caseificio Masi
via Mazzini 195/199
Ostuni
T: +39 0831 30 33 44

To a passer-by the Latticini Masi shop seems to be only a small establishment situated right next to a petrol station. Its regular customers, however, know that this modest retail front houses Caseificio Masi, the company that churns out (quite literally) cheese for discerning buyers — and that includes some of the region's best restaurants.

The shop certainly gets busy but that's nothing to the frantic activity in the production area hidden behind it. Gianni Orlandino, who has worked here for 13 years, explains: "The cheese makers start at 2am, go through to 10 or 11am and the first trucks are loaded up at 5am." Only local milk is used, but the Masi cheeses don't just stay in Puglia. They travel throughout Italy, and to Greece and France.

Caciocavallo is Gianni's favourite cheese, and it's one that even has legal status with its own *Denominazione di Origine Controllata* (DOC). Made to order and weighing 1.5 kgs, each cheese must mature for at least 60 days and is individually branded with a heated iron. But Masi produces many other Pugliese specialities too: ricotta, *scamorza*, mozzarella, *fior di latte*, *cacioricotta*, *stracciatella* and of course one of the great food experiences of Puglia: *burrata*.

Masi sells over a hundred 300g *burrata* each day — not least because they have a short shelf life. The *burrata* maker uses flat pats of *fior di latte*, which looks like mozzarella, but is made from cows' milk. He then deftly wraps these around strings of the cheese and rich cream (*stracciatella*).

If you really want to prove yourself to the Pugliese, finish a *burrata* on your own. Gianni states, with some pride, that "here in Puglia, we'll have a *burrata* each, whereas in the north, they share one between five. We have big appetites here in the south."

Agrinatura Giancarlo Ceci: Organic Agriculture

Agrinatura Giancarlo Ceci
C.da Sant Agostino
70031 Andria
www.agrinatura.net

Giancarlo Ceci's farm has been in his family for eight generations. There have been many changes in that 200-year period, but one of the biggest was also one of the most recent. As a student at the University of Bologna, Giancarlo was part of an acknowledged hothouse of progressive agricultural thinking. As a result he was one of the first farmers in Puglia to enter into large-scale organic farming.

That was back in 1988. Today Agrinatura Giancarlo Ceci is a huge success producing, in the main, a wide range of vegetables such as cabbage, broccoli, cauliflower, tomatoes, fennel, celery, chard and some salad leaves and fruit such as melon, cherries, watermelon, a few plums and table grapes.

And then there are the bottles. Some contain Giancarlo's olive oil, a deep golden coloured liquid whose organic origins are evident in the unmistakeable taste of *territorio*: fruity and rich though never overpowering. As for the wine, he is excited about the prospects of his 70 hectares of vines but he's well aware that this project cannot be rushed. "Producing good wine takes time," he says. "One has to be patient and calm, especially in the early years." The chardonnay *en barrique* is a personal favourite, but his reds are receiving increasing recognition: his Castel del Monte DOC Rosso 'Parco Marano' 2004 was given a Diploma di Gran Menzione at Vinitaly in 2006.

Organic farming is not the only example of his forward thinking. Energy issues are another focus. "Clean energy is a major concern for us," he says. Solar panels are not viable ("the required panels would be huge") so the preferred energy source is biomass. "We're aiming to be self-sufficient," he says. He certainly managed to achieve that with irrigation: in the late 1980s artesian wells were excavated to leave the farm less at the mercy of frequent droughts.

With 200 years of family history in one farm you might think that Giancarlo would feel the heavy weight of tradition on his shoulders. But ancient and modern coexist comfortably on Giancarlo's farm. He may live in a centuries-old castle, but his streamlined modern office in its grounds is state of the art. Documents showing the family's aristocratic heritage and framed accounting ledgers from 1899–1908 hang next to recently awarded certificates. And, alongside modern machinery, there are a couple of horses working the fields.

This is no nostalgic embellishment but an old tradition with a very relevant application to modern farming. Giancarlo explains: "The two working horses are useful in the cultivation of vines and produce such as broccoli because a horse can get much nearer to the plants than a machine, without causing any damage."

The man who currently cares for and handles the horses has also inspired two of his sons to carry on in his footsteps. And that continuation through the generations is a frequent occurrence on Giancarlo's farm. Tommaso, a delightful man who manages the teams of workers when not getting his hands dirty realigning irrigation pipes and checking on produce, has worked there his whole life, as did his father and his grandfather before him. Giancarlo has fond memories of Tommaso's grandfather but then so does Tommaso's family of his. In fact Giancarlo in his turn is liked and respected not only by his workers and peers but, it seems, everyone in the area you speak to.

So will Giancarlo's children follow in his footsteps? "Time will tell," he says. "I can only hope that my children will develop a natural passion for this farm in the way that my father ensured that it developed spontaneously within me. He never forced the issue. I, in my turn, won't have it any other way."

Antonio Buccarella: Ionian Gamberoni

Antonio (Tony) Buccarella
via Trieste 135
73014 Gallipoli

At 3am we arrived at Gallipoli port. We set sail at 3.30. It was almost pitch black.

Travelling with captain Tony Buccarella and his crew — brothers Salvatore and Danilo — it took us two and a half hours to reach our fishing destination. At 6am the fishing nets went down. The cords are some 250 metres long and the speed at which they roll round the wheels causes huge friction and big clouds of acrid smoke. The nets stay down for six hours. This is not recreational fishing.

Today, it's a good catch: 60kg of *gamberoni*. Other fish are returned to the sea, apart from whatever is chosen for lunch, and the *gamberoni* are sorted by size. Tony prefers scampi, but the *gamberoni* fetch the best prices; he only wishes he could catch more.

He certainly puts in the hours. We dock at 7pm, returning well after all the other boats. As soon as we're safely docked, he rushes off to the wholesale Gallipoli fish market; a fair part of his haul has already been sold to restaurateurs who have been calling him on our approach to port. Tony's catch sells so quickly in fact that he has time to relax for a few minutes and chat with his peers at the fish market. But he's soon back to the boat to check that Salvatore and Danilo have filled it up with fuel, that there are enough recycled polystyrene boxes and that there are no problems. Tony's boat is called Cristina, after both his mother and the patron saint of Gallipoli. Cristina has always taken care of Tony and his crew.

The other woman in Tony's life waits for him on the quay. Tony and Francesca were married five years ago, having been together for 14 years . It was a long wait, but Francesca is understanding. "He had to buy the boat, then the house, and save for the wedding," she says, adding: "But I know the boat's the most important thing to him." "I never say that," counters Tony. Francesca smiles. "He doesn't need to."

Taralli della Regina

Taralli della Regina
Di Benedictis Giovanna
via Miciaccia 8
Palo del Colle
T: +39 080 627 475

Taralli are a delicious Pugliese bread speciality. Little rings (or knots or a number of other shapes) of dough, they can be crunchy and substantial, or very short — and very moreish. Particularly popular as snacks and as an accompaniment to antipasto platters, they are found in most bread baskets.

Classic *taralli* dough is made with flour, olive oil, white wine, salt and yeast only, but fennel seeds are a popular addition. In fact there are a number of variations such as onion, chilli, sesame and anchovy. The dough is mixed, rolled, shaped and then plunged into boiling water for 20-30 seconds before being baked at 170°C for an hour. Giovanna Di Benedictis, who set up the firm Taralli della Regina in Palo del Colle over a decade ago, says that the plunge into boiling water is necessary because "it makes them crumbly. And," she adds, "because it's tradition."

She also explains that the amount of yeast required changes depending on the ambient temperature. That goes for the working hours, too. Her small team works from 5am through to 2pm Monday to Saturday in winter. But they only work Monday to Friday in summer as it gets too hot.

Giovanna's is one of 20-odd *taralli-making* businesses in this small town alone, but there are numerous individuals who prepare batches for their friends and families at home, some using their nearest baker's oven to cook them. Yet even at Taralli della Regina, which is clearly a commercial operation, making 150kg of *taralli* a day and selling throughout Puglia, all the *taralli* forming is done by hand. Another nod to tradition, perhaps. Then again, it's done pretty quickly, or as Giovanna briskly puts it: "You need dextrous hands to work here."

Azienda Agricola Taurino Cosimo: Wine

Azienda Agricola Taurino
Cosimo
73010 Guagnano
T: +39 0832 706 490
www.taurinovini.it

Open: Sept–Jun 08.00–13.00
and 15.00–17.00; Jul–Aug
08.00–13.00
Public tastings welcomed but
reservation essential.

Forty years ago, Pugliese wines weren't taken seriously. Most producers sent their wine to the north of Italy to be lost in blends. One of these was Francesco Taurino. But Cosimo, his son, had long reasoned that if his father's wine was good enough to 'improve' other people's, then it should be able to stand alone.

Even after he had graduated, become a pharmacist, married Rita and started a family, Cosimo constantly yearned to return to the vines and change things. In 1970 he quietly set aside a few barrels which were bottled in their own right. Back then, Cosimo had few supporters but was determined to convert the sceptics. Rita still smiles when remembering the early struggles: washing bottles by hand, filling them from a jug and sticking on labels by hand into the early hours.

The breakthrough came in 1974, when the jewel in the Taurino crown was created: Patriglione, which in competition was acknowledged to be one of the best wines in Italy. Now nothing could hold back Cosimo — or his wines. Word spread and overseas orders started to arrive, especially from the USA. Over the years things have progressed and technology helps: for example, ceiling sensors above the oak barrels detect when humidity drops below a programmed level and trigger a waterfall. It's a long way from scrubbing bottles and sticking on labels.

Unfortunately the great Cosimo died before the next phase of his vineyard but he did see both his adored children, Francesco and Rosanna, enter the business. In fact, if you don't speak Italian, Rosanna will probably be the one to guide you through a tasting. Today, almost four decades after the first thousand bottles, the company produces almost a million a year, of which 800,000 are exported. No wonder Rita is proud of how much they've achieved. Does she have a favourite Taurino wine? "I don't — I can't. They're all my children."

Clockwise from top:
Local women working in the
Taurino fields.

Rita Taurino invites Vittorio
Cavaliere, a highly-regarded wine
dealer, to share his thoughts on
the latest Taurino reds.

Wine barrels in the new Azienda.

Alberobello

Miseriaenobiltà

At the bottom of Via Monte San Michele is
Largo Martellotta. Cross over this and climb
the steps to the RHS of Via Acquaviva (a faint
sign shows Via Contessa Acquaviva). At the
top of the steps, carry straight ahead to reach
Piazza del Popolo. Hug the wall round to your
left and Miseriaenobiltà is on your left.

Andria

De la Poste, Locanda

Go down Corso Cavour (from the railway line
towards the historic centre). On arriving at a
major crossroads (junction with Via Alcide De
Gaspari), go right down Via Giovanni Bovio.
Continue along here until you reach the Post
Office on RHS (shown by a yellow circle with
a blue 'PT') next to Via XX Settembre, a small
one-way street. Opposite this on LHS is De
la Poste, Locanda. If you reach the tree and
landscaped park/roundabout of Piazza
Umberto 1°, you've gone too far.

Or, from Piazza Vittorio Emanuele II, go down
Via Porta Castello to the same junction with
Corso Cavour (etc see above) and go left down
Via Giovanni Bovio.

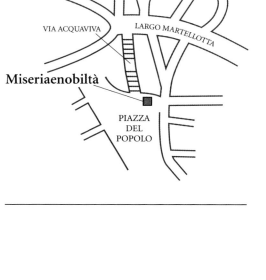

Andria-Montegrosso

Antichi Sapori

From Andria, take the SP231 to Canosa.
Montegrosso is well signposted. And when
you reach the T-junction which is the town,
go to your right, and Antichi Sapori is there
on your right.

Bari

Il Pane e le Rose

From Corso Vittorio Emanuele (the main drag), at the top end of Piazza Libertà (the car park in front of the Palazzo del Governo), turn down Via Roberto da Bari and continue. Just after Via Principe Amedeo is Il Pane e le Rose on LHS.

PerBacco

Just past Il Pane e le Rose, turn left down Via Dante Alighieri at the next junction. Continue until reaching the big Corso Cavour. Cross straight over this and continue (at this point the road becomes Via Imbriani). Continue straight ahead (you are heading towards the waterfront with the sea also on LHS). Turn left down Via Francesco Saverio Abbrescia, and a short way down on RHS is PerBacco, with two lamps outside.

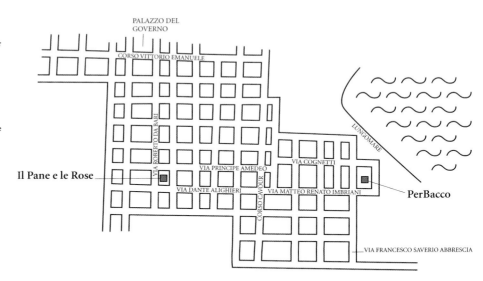

Brindisi

Trattoria Pantagruele

From Piazza Vittorio Emanuele II on the waterfront (at the end of Corso Garibaldi), walk away from the water up the RHS of the Piazza, and at the corner carry straight ahead (with the Banca d'Italia to your LHS) up Via Filomeno Consiglio. Pass two small roads on your RHS and then on your right is a small square: Salita di Ripalta, with the green awnings of Pantagruele.

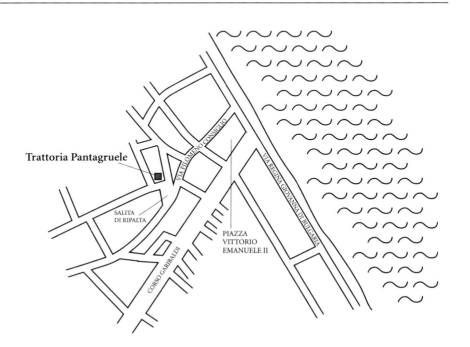

Carovigno

Osteria Già Sotto L'Arco

Go along Corso Vittorio Emanuele until it opens up into a square. There is a monument to Caduti II Guerra Mondiale 1940-45 on RHS, and opposite this is the restaurant on LHS. In front of you is the Chiesa del Carmine, and straight ahead on LHS is a statue of Padre Pio.

Ceglie Messapica

Al Fornello da Ricci

(Not shown on map).
From the Santuario S. Rocco, go left to Taranto. At the end of the road, still following signs for Taranto, go left down the small Via Pasquale Mancini, and then right to Taranto. Carry straight on to a park, and continue to the left, still following signs for Taranto. At the junction (roundabout with a petrol station) carry straight on towards Villa Castelli. The road widens, there is a sign to Montevicoli and a right turn to Martina Franca, with a yellow sign indicating Al Fornello da Ricci. Carry along here for a short way, then follow another yellow sign for the restaurant, left up a small country road.

A short way along here is a small sign of the restaurant on the LHS, and it is right in front of you up a narrow track, approximately 2km from the Santuario.

Cibus

From Piazza Plebiscito, take Via Giuseppe Elia (directly opposite Corso Garibaldi), signposted for Chiesa Matrice and Cibus. Continue along Via Giuseppe Elia (road bears round to left) and turn right at second road on right, just before reaching the Church, on to Via Giuseppe elia Gia Municipio. Continue down the gentle steps of this road and the Cibus sign is in front of you for the restaurant and wine bar on RHS.

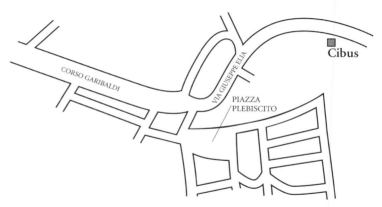

Conversano

Pashà

In Piazza Castello, with Castle on LHS and garden on RHS, Pashà is on the corner and on the edge of Piazza della Conciliazione.

Foggia

Chacaito

From Piazza XX Settembre, cross over Corso G. Garibaldi and walk down Via Duomo towards the old town and the cathedral. Walk across Piazza del Lago, passing the cathedral on RHS. Cross over Piazza Card. P Felici then continue straight ahead across Piazza F de Sanctis until reaching a junction with Via Arpi. Turn right (noting that straight ahead is Vico Peschi which leads to the market), and after a short while Chacaito is on LHS.

Chacaito, Osteria Zio Aldo

PIAZZA MERCATO

VICO PESCHI

VIA ARPI

CATTEDRALE

PIAZZA DEL LAGO

PIAZZA F DE SANCTIS

PIAZZA CARD. P FELICI

CORSO G. GARIBALDI

VIA DUOMO

PIAZZA XX SETTEMBRE

Gallipoli

La Puritate

Walk down the main road, Corso Roma, towards the old town. Continue over the bridge (Ponte Città Vecchia) passing the castle on LHS and then the fish market on RHS. At the top of the bridge/castle ramp, take the first right along the waterfront, Riviera Cristoforo Colombo, which becomes the Riviera Nazario Sauro at the corner. Continue. On RHS is the sea. Next to the Chiesa della Purità on LHS at the end of Via Sant'Elia is the dark wooden conservatory of La Puritate restaurant.

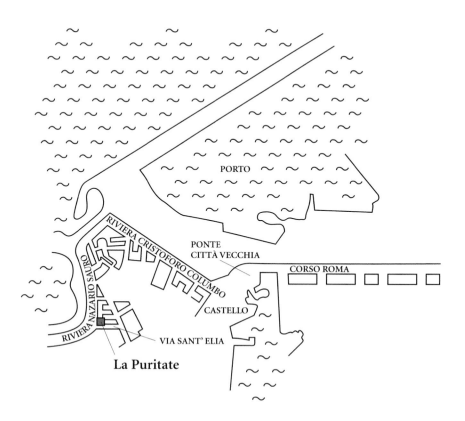

PORTO

RIVIERA CRISTOFORO COLUMBO

RIVIERA NAZARIO SAURO

PONTE CITTÀ VECCHIA

CORSO ROMA

CASTELLO

VIA SANT' ELIA

La Puritate

Lecce

Alle Due Corti

From in front of the Chiesa del Gesù (Piazza Castromediano), with the church on your LHS, take the road straight ahead, (Via Francesco Rubichi), passing Via Oronzo Tiso on your LHS.

After the crossroads (Via Francesco Antonio D'Amelio on RHS, and Via degli Antoglietta on LHS), the road becomes Via Leonardo Prato. Shortly after this are two small dead ends on RHS: Corte dei Ziani and Corte Giugni, and between these two is Alle Due Corti.

Cucina Casereccia

From the Chiesa di Santa Croce, walk through the Preffetura/Monastero dei Celestini and cross Via XXV Luglio into the public gardens. Continue into the centre of the gardens to the column and turn left, past the children's play area. Exit the gardens on LHS, through the gate to your left, and cross over Via Garibaldi using the traffic island. Turn left and take the first road on your right, hugging the wall so that you take the right and not the left fork. The road straight ahead is Via Colonello A Costadura. Continue along this passing Via Di Porcigliano on RHS and Via Di Casanella, again on RHS. On RHS is a blue vertical sign saying Trattoria with a red sign beneath, Cucina Casereccia.

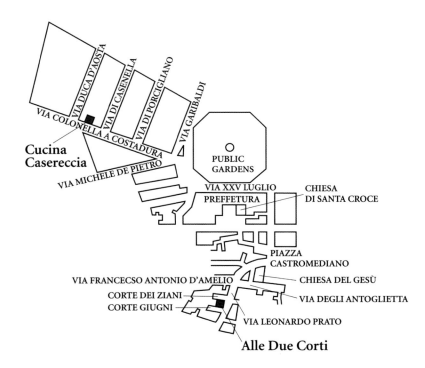

Martina Franca

Ciacco

From Piazza Immacolata go down Via Garibaldi, past Caffè Tripoli on LHS and straight ahead into a narrow road, Via Poerio. The road bears to the left, becoming Via Ageslao Milano. Carry on and the road leads into a very small square called Piazzetta Conte Ugolino. At the end of this, turn right at the T-junction and Ciacco is a few steps in front of you.

Il Ritrovo degli Amici

From Piazza XX Settembre, walk away from the Arco di Sant'Antonio down Corso Messapia which runs to the LHS of the small public garden in front of the church – Piazzetta S.Antonio. Carry along here and a few shops along on the RHS is the iron gate and steps of Il Ritrovo degli Amici. It's diagonally opposite Via Ennio (on the LHS). If you reach Via Antonio Bruno on your RHS, you've gone too far and need to go back a couple of doors.

Monopoli

Lido Bianco

From Piazza XX Settembre (where a lively market is held to a backdrop of Chiesa S Domenico Con Rosone) walk along Via Indelli until you reach Piazza (G. le) D'Annunzio (actually just a largish traffic junction). Turn left here and carry on all the way down Via Cadorna towards the sea. Just before the sea, in front of the car park, turn right down Via Procaccia (Lido Bianco is signposted here). Just past a small patch of grass with trees is a small road to the left (again with a sign to 'Ristorante Lido Bianco'). The restaurant car park is immediately on the left; a short way further down the road is the water's edge, a small but very popular beach and the restaurant.

Monte Sant'Angelo

La Taverna Li Jalantuúmene

Stand in front of the Basilica di San Michele Arcangelo with your back to the iron-fenced square. Diagonally in front of you are steps leading down to the Tomba di Rotari; go down these and then another set to your left. In front of you is the Battistero di San Giovanni in Tumba. Continue down to the right, down further steps beneath a house, and in front of you is a sign "Taverna di Li Jalantuúmene" with an arrow to the left indicating a Trattoria. Continue past a few houses until reaching Piazza De Galganis on RHS, with the Chiesa S.S Trinità. Immediately on your right as you enter the Piazza is the Taverna.

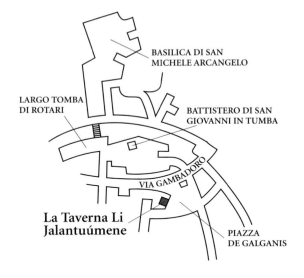

Orsara di Puglia

Peppe Zullo

From the centre of Orsara, take the road to Troia. Upon leaving town there is a Peppe Zullo sign on the corner (although it can be difficult to see from this direction); turn left just after a blue and white "Arredamenti Zulli Mobili" sign. The restaurant is a short way up here and is signposted. A grassy spot on RHS is used as a car park. There's a large entrance through which is another car park for those staying overnight, and the restaurant entrance is to the left of this – a wooden door at the end of a foliage-covered tunnel.

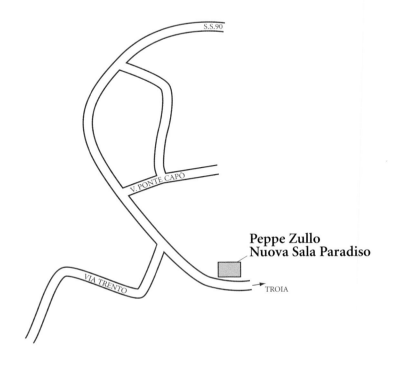

Polignano a Mare

Da Tuccino

From Piazza Aldo Moro, head west to Piazza Garibaldi and continue straight ahead on Via S. Vito past Via Conversano on RHS. The road bears round to the left past Largo Gelso on RHS. Carry straight on Via S. Vito out of town towards Bari and after a couple of kilometres you'll see a small sign indicating a sharp turn right to Da Tuccino. The car park is a short way down this narrow road and the restaurant is on LHS overlooking the sea.

Trani

Osteria Corteinfiore

At Piazza della Libertà take the right fork, namely Via Ognissanti and continue along past the fish market on LHS (Piazza Campo dei Longobardi). The road winds somewhat, and shortly after going under a bridge formed by a house over the street, there are two large wooden doors on LHS and the sign announcing Osteria Corteinfiore.

Torrente Antico

From Piazza della Repubblica, go past the grey-fronted Laboratorio/Farmacia on the corner down Via Mario Pagano. The first road on LHS is very narrow (just past Via S. Maria on RHS) and is Via Edoardo Fusco, just in front of the triangular Piazza Libertà. Turn down this and just past the metal road blocks on LHS is the dark green awning and entrance of Ristorante Torrente Antico.

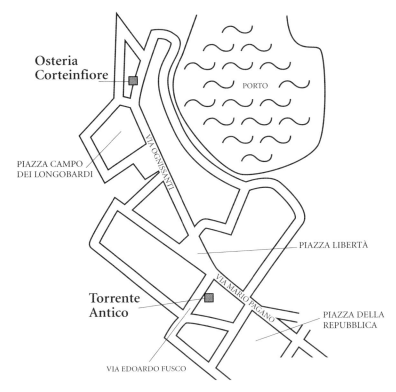

Index

Acknowledgements

The author would like to thank: everybody who has helped with the research and completion of this book, especially everyone in Puglia, for their warm welcomes and runaway enthusiasm for our project; continued gratitude to my husband Dan, a constant inspiration and support, and so much more fun than I probably deserve; the brilliant and inventive Bonny Day Publishing, especially Elizabeth Canning, who so generously shares her expertise, Andrea Bothamley for meticulous attention to detail and Dan Bertauche, who troubleshoots with panache; my editor, Vaughan O'Grady who calmly, sensitively and good humouredly held my hand through the painful process of halving the amount of copy that finally made it to print; the recipe testers, Pete Livesey, Carol O'Shea and Susan Searle, for painstaking work; Franco Taruschio for his kindness and encouragement; Cathy Colecchi for providing ever-dependable support from the USA; Massimo Rotoloni and Sara Sacchetti for Italian help in London; Vittorio Cavaliere, "Mr Puglia", for taking me under his wing and pointing me in the right direction with his invaluable insider info; Giancarlo Ceci for being a magnanimous and inspiring individual; Carole and Mino Maggi for ensuring that we were comfortable and rested and whose cooking school is a blast; Pasquale Centrone for always making us feel happy and for his tenacity in organising a fishing trip, despite the amount of red tape involved; Robert Collins and Lili Okuyama for road testing the final draft with such gusto; Adam Morley for endless great ideas; Pete Dawson and Tegan Danko at Grade Design for yet another elegant and seductive design solution and for indispensable practical help; Peter O'Shea for adding lateral thinking to proceedings, liberally sprinkled with Irish wit and charm; Caroline Shaw and Jane Livesey for unwavering support and the best nights out; Ted Gush for being "Papà Gusto"; Dave Bone for tirelessly ensuring that the new Appetites office is both a green and happy place to work; and Eddie Jacob, who has an extraordinary ability to concentrate on the job in hand in the midst of complete chaos and uncertainty, who unfailingly produces stunning and surprising images, and who can delightfully see the funny side of confusion as readily as he can see an opportunistic shot across a crowded piazza. I have no idea how he manages it but I'm overjoyed that he does.

The photographer would like to thank: the Pugliesi, for a seemingly endless enthusiasm, pride and desire to show us all that this very special region has to offer. From the humblest fisherman to the most renowned chefs, we were met with open arms and with a passion so moving that it was an unforgettable experience. The photographs couldn't help but – almost – create themselves as proof of such a tradition of hospitality, honesty and creativity. I hope those concerned see this reflected in the pictures that lay within these pages.

Thanks to everyone at Bonny Day Publishing for all their support and yet another opportunity to experience the delights of one of Europe's most magical cultures. And lastly, thank you to Christine for being yet again the best travelling companion a photographer could possibly wish for. It was indeed another fantastic adventure.